W9-BKC-163

"Dick Richards brings together the key strands for business success and personal growth. If Peter Block's *Stewardship* explains the 'how,' then *Artful Work* explains the 'why.' I have enjoyed and learned much from this book. It will be required reading for all chief executives in our leadership programs."

—Eric Thompson, Director of Executive Programs,
University of Ulster Business School

"Dick Richards offers challenging insights on how to exercise artful leadership, create a centered organization, see all work as spiritual work."

—*Working from the Heart*

"Elegant . . . Richards looks to the world of art for inspiration about the nature of work . . . a book that will resonate for those who are already open to its holistic language and message. Those readers who aren't should read it anyway—maybe it will crack that deadened, mechanical vision of work that slipped in with the Industrial Age."

—*Quality Digest*

"Wouldn't it be great if we could stop separating 'work' from 'life' and find a way to make it a more fulfilling part of our lives? Richards introduces a method for returning passion and commitment to the workplace . . . an innovative approach to a popular theme."

—*NAPRA ReVIEW*

"Compact, provocative, and inspirational . . . Mr. Richards gently escorts the reader into the new realm of work where artistry is once again united with industry."

—*Industry Week*

"A thought-provoking case for rethinking our view of work . . . inspirational as well as practical."

—*Ethical Management*

"Lively reflections on how to derive joy and meaning from the workplace."

—*The Bookwatch*

"Artfully written."

—*The Cincinnati Post*

Most Berkley Books are available at special quantity discounts for bulk purchases for sales promotions, premiums, fund-raising, or educational use. Special books or book excerpts can also be created to fit specific needs.

For details, write to Special Markets, The Berkley Publishing Group, 200 Madison Avenue, New York, New York 10016.

ARTFUL
WORK

*Awakening Joy, Meaning, and Commitment
in the Workplace*

Dick Richards

BERKLEY BOOKS, NEW YORK

ARTFUL WORK

A Berkley Book / published by arrangement with
the author

PRINTING HISTORY
Berrett-Koehler Publishers edition published 1995
Berkley trade paperback edition / July 1997

All rights reserved.
Copyright © 1995 by Dick Richards.
This book may not be reproduced in whole or in part,
by mimeograph or any other means, without permission.
For information address: The Berkley Publishing Group,
200 Madison Avenue, New York, New York 10016.

The Putnam Berkley World Wide Web site address is
http://www.berkley.com

ISBN: 0-425-15914-0

BERKLEY®
Berkley Books are published by The Berkley Publishing Group.
200 Madison Avenue, New York, New York 10016.
BERKLEY and the "B" design
are trademarks belonging to Berkley Publishing Corporation.

PRINTED IN THE UNITED STATES OF AMERICA

10 9 8 7 6 5 4 3 2 1

To

Bobbi V, who brought smiles and love on this journey,

and to

the people of Camphill Village Kimberton Hills,

who remind me to cherish wonder

CONTENTS

CONTENTS

PREFACE

As I write this, a brisk wind disturbs the tall oaks and hemlocks surrounding my home. The treetops dance like flames caught in puffs of breath. I try to recall why I pledged these words to paper. I attend to the wind and it offers recollections.

My first recollections are of Christmases, Easters, and Thanksgivings — times when my family gathers. My father and his brother, my uncle, separate themselves from the rest of us. They sit in a den, or on a patio, alone together. Their voices carry beyond the space they have carved for themselves.

My father is the night-shift foreman for a steel-forging company. My uncle is vice-president of the company. They talk and argue lovingly, as caring brothers will. I, as a child or teenager, don't understand the issues that compel them, but I do experience the passion and commitment in their voices. I begin to comprehend that work means something more than earning a paycheck.

This book supports our wish to bring passion and commitment to all of our work and to create workplaces that honor those qualities. It is to stimulate courageous and hopeful aspects of ourselves which seek to make our work lives more joyful, fruitful, and productive.

I recall also Ansel Adams, the extraordinary photographer, speaking of the moment when he first realized that he was not taking pictures of objects; rather, he was capturing light. Film sees only light. This realization led

Adams to perceive his work in a new and vastly more rewarding way. His novel perception unlocked his greatness. We can all gain something new and more exhilarating from our work and in our organizations. Perhaps we too can achieve greatness.

This book offers a new and more rewarding way of perceiving all of our work as well as our organizations. Its primary purpose is to enrich our view of the work we do and of the places where we do our work.

The wind also brings memories of my own history. I have always been fascinated with the process of creating art. My first career was as a graphic artist. During the years since I abandoned that career, I have dabbled in drawing, painting, photography, filmmaking, poetry, writing, and music. Sometimes I view my "dabbling" with disdain — the ramblings of someone who cannot commit to one course. At other times I see my ramblings with more compassion. They are perhaps the experiments of one who is interested more in the *process* of art than in any one artistic endeavor.

In recent years my fascination led me to a more careful study of artistry and to the belief that all work can become artful — artfulness is the key to passion and commitment. And, like Adams, whether our work is artful depends more on how we perceive our work than on the work itself. As a consultant to organizations, I also began to sense that artfulness is a core component of organizational success.

I present two primary concepts in this book: artful work and organizational centering. Artful work embodies different ways of perceiving ourselves and the work we do. Organizational centering concerns how we perceive the workplaces we create and what we do there. We will begin with artful work

then explore organizational centering. As in any story with two main charac-
ters, in the end we will probe the relationship between the two.

The first eight chapters describe the beliefs of artful work, which are
designed as an invitation to be who we are in our endeavors. Chapter 9
explores organizational centering, a way to bring the fullness of our humanity
to our workplaces. In the last section of chapter 9, Characteristics of a
Centered Organization, I attempt to weave together the relationship between
artful work and organizational centering, forming an overarching summary
of the book. Chapter 10 concerns artful leadership. While all work holds the
potential for artfulness, leadership absolutely requires it because leadership
concerns vision, creativity, and spirit.

The principal image for understanding both artful work and organizational centering is that of an artist seated at a potter's wheel. The image
comes from M. C. Richards's seminal work, *Centering: In Pottery, Poetry, and
the Person* (1989). M. C. views herself as a "sower of seeds." She most
certainly sowed the seeds for this book. They are scattered throughout.
(Although M. C. and I share the same last name, we are not related — at
least not biologically. Perhaps spiritually.)

Each chapter begins with a brief quotation from M. C.'s book. *Artful
Work* also contains forms inspired by her pottery. She wrote that "any bowl is
symbolic of an archetypal circular form. . . ." (1989, 20). These forms
include circles, which symbolize the self and the ultimate wholeness of life;
spirals, which emanate from and return to a center at the same time; and
labyrinths, which define and protect their center. The forms are included
here to call up continually the image of centering and to remind us that work

that emerges from our own center is the most artful work we can do.

Artful Work has many subtexts. One is to bring together two estranged siblings: art and science. Art concerns vision, emotion, spirit, and soul. Science deals with technique and rational inquiry. Our tendency has been to view them as separate entities. In our work and organizational lives, we have immersed ourselves in science and forfeited the fulfillment that artfulness can bring. My hope is that the ideas in this book will enable us to end that forfeiture.

Another subtext is the imperative of finding new vision as a precondition for making a success of new technique. I do not offer techniques here. We have enough technique! We don't have sufficient vision or passion about the vision we do have. Sufficient vision and passion will arise from artfulness, and when they do, we will invent any technique we lack.

A third subtext is the need to trust our own inner voices and gauges. In that spirit I want to echo the words of an early-twentieth-century painter and art teacher, Robert Henri, who wrote, "Don't take me as an authority. I am simply expressing a very personal point of view. Nothing final about it. You have to settle all these matters for yourself" (1984, 129).

I hope *Artful Work* is a brisk wind — a wind that delivers new meaning to our work, whatever it may be, and spurs all of us to create workplaces that inspire artfulness.

Albrightsville, Pennsylvania   Dick Richards
December 1994

ACKNOWLEDGMENTS

A book uses many people to create itself. It needs ideas, criticism, technical expertise, and nurturing. An author does not know many of the people his own book calls upon.

I do know that the people and groups listed here contributed in significant ways to this book. I am grateful to all of them.

I want to thank three people especially. Steven Piersanti published this book. Without his dedication to bringing new ideas forward, it would not be alive.

M. C. Richards's wonderful writing about centering provided the image around which the book revolves.

Susan Smyth's dedication to truth telling helped keep me honest.

John Adams
Bill Dickinson
Ray Doughty
Sarah Engel
Carol Frenier
Marvin Israelow
Mike Jackson
Caira Maguire
Marie Morgan
Warren Osborne
Steven Piersanti

M. C. Richards
Bill Scharf
Patti Schroeder
Barbara Shipka
Susan Smyth
Melissa Stratton
Shelley Sweet
Eric Thompson
David Trickett
Barbara Voros
Diana Whitney

The people of
Camphill Village
Kimberton Hills
Various artists from
Allentown, Pennsylvania
Participants in the
International Directors
Program at the
University of Ulster
Business School
The staff and associates
of Berrett-Koehler

THE ORDERS DON'T WORK ANYMORE

1

The birth of the new entails the death of the old, change.

In the fable, *The Little Prince*, Antoine de Saint-Exupéry wrote of a lamplighter who lived and worked on a tiny planet that turned more rapidly from year to year until the time came when a day lasted only a minute. The lamplighter followed orders. His orders determined his way of working and required that he light his one lamp at dusk and then extinguish it at dawn. Once each minute, the lamplighter lit his lamp and then extinguished it.

"I follow a terrible profession," the lamplighter told the little prince. "In the old days it was reasonable. I put the lamp out in the morning, and in the evening I lighted it again. I had the rest of the day for relaxation and the rest of the night for sleep."

The little prince, puzzled by the lamplighter's behavior and not yet noticing the brevity of the days, asked, "And the orders have been changed since that time?"

"The orders have not been changed," the lamplighter replied. "That is the tragedy! From year to year the planet has turned more rapidly and the orders have not been changed!" (1971, 48)

CHANGING OUR BELIEFS

Those of us who tinker with work and workplaces — executives, managers, consultants — are, like the lamplighter, following outdated orders based on questionable beliefs about our world. Our orders describe what we actually *do*. Our beliefs are what we accept as true. Orders evolve from beliefs.

Our present-day orders evolved from the beliefs of traditional Newtonian science, which form the "old paradigm," or the "Newtonian paradigm," about which we have read and heard so much in the last few years. The beliefs include:

- Objectivity is possible
- The world is arranged hierarchically
- Change occurs through evolution
- The cause of events can be understood as a linear, mechanical process
- Nature can be understood in a rational way by manipulating it in experiments

- **Nature can be controlled and dominated**
- **The world we know is "out there" and we are "in here" in a separate and distinct way**
- **Truth, the whole truth, can be known**

The force of the evidence that these beliefs are inadequate is overcoming our inevitable human resistance to change. Our world, like the lamplighter's, is not what it used to be. It is changing faster and faster, and the world of work and business is changing with it.

Management consultant Peter Vaill described our situation as "permanent white water" (1989, 2). It is an apt image that conjures swirling forces eager to engulf us. Yet we are resilient beings, capable of coping and even thriving under difficult circumstances. We can rise to challenges. Some of us even seek white water. We can also view the world anew, reinventing ourselves. Current times demand that we have those capabilities.

Our familiar beliefs also cause us to embrace a never-ending procession of techniques. We have tried managing by objectives, searching for excellence, creating vision statements, self-managing teams, instituting notions about quality and service, and now reengineering. We spin from one solution to the next, and our solutions are too often ineffective because they address the symptoms rather than the causes. The problem is that we change our ideas and techniques without changing our beliefs.

We have also been trying to learn from one another for far too long. We are lamplighters learning from other lamplighters, caught in the same beliefs. We have unwittingly created a cycle in which we reinforce one another, decry our lack of progress toward real change, and go on doing what we have

3

always done. We often say the same things in different words and do the same things using new words, yielding only ephemeral results. We tell one another when and how to light the lamp. We notice that the world has changed forever but allow the depth of change to register only in some murky recess of our mind. And we continue to follow the old orders and hold on to the old beliefs.

The lamplighter was a dedicated man who wanted simply to do his work as best he could. We too are dedicated people, most of us, struggling and floundering, as humans will when the world is disorienting, as if we are in an amusement park fun house.

This book is about work, organizations, management, and leadership. However, because we need to question our current beliefs and orders, I draw very little from what we typically think of as management science. Instead I am inspired by artists: novelists, poets, potters, painters, and other people who are sometimes considered oddballs by those of us who inhabit organizational corridors. Artists embrace different beliefs and orders and see work differently than do most people who work in organizations. We have much to learn from them.

MANY LENSES

I am slowly picking my way along the rocky bank of the Mud Run, one of the finest trout-fishing streams in the Pocono Mountains of Pennsylvania. I am not carrying my favorite fly rod this morning; instead I am hauling a camera, a tripod, and a half-dozen lenses. I am once again in search of the ideal photograph.

The photograph I seek has eluded me for almost twenty-five years. Stubbornly, I resist the urge to examine why. Is it because I am a poor photographer, or because of my occasional ruinous perfectionism, or because the ideal photograph simply does not exist? Perhaps I will not allow it to exist because, if it did, my search would be over. A friend once said, "I hope my dreams don't all come true. What would life be without dreams?"

5

The light is flawless; splendid, early morning light filtered by trees and mist. A small oak, perhaps a foot tall, perches in a bed of emerald moss atop a rock in the middle of the stream. The rock seems a precarious home. I can imagine the tree many years from now, with thick roots embracing the rock, anchored in the streambed below.

I set up my tripod on the bank of the stream, attach the camera, choose a long lens. The tiny tree is about twelve feet away. Point, focus, shoot. Again, sliding the lens to gain a different view: point, focus, shoot. Then again.

I want to be closer to this courageous, fledgling tree. The distance between us feels restraining. The edge of the water is a barrier. I want to see the tree through a shorter lens, perhaps even a macro lens. I will have to suffer the quick, cold, shallow water. This process of seeing through many lenses has become vital to me, not only in photography but also in life and work. My need often causes me inconvenience and discomfort; and sometimes I have to get wet.

As people who are interested in organizations that are struggling in a changing business universe, the more lenses we have, the more flexible we can be when looking at the issues confronting us. We need macro lenses to examine what is close to us. We need wide-angle lenses to register the breadth of our horizons. We need zoom lenses to capture the images and dreams that occupy the distant future. The more lenses in our bag, the better our chance of creating a sparkling picture.

I suspect we will peer through a lot of lenses as we explore and embrace new beliefs about work and business — beliefs that fit both ourselves and our times. We might have to get wet along the way; and we might have to suffer some discomfort.

BORROWING A LENS

The fundamental substance of organizations is the energy of people. That energy is like the clay a potter shapes, the pigment a painter wields, or the words a poet applies to images. When we organize or reorganize companies today, we usually think about things such as centralization and decentralization, corporate architecture, reengineering, spans of control, and market segments. In other words, we think about everything except people's energy, the fundamental substance.

Along with examining our beliefs about the energy of people, we will all benefit from examining our notions about the nature of work itself. Most work involves the interaction between people and human organizations. Work is an essential channel for our energies; it is one way we find ourselves and one way we contribute our energy to the world.

Organizations crave work; people furnish work.

HUMAN ENERGY → WORK → ORGANIZATIONS

Perhaps we can borrow a lens from people who regularly study things such as work and human energy. We have much to learn from those whose perspective is different from our own.

Who are the people who see the world differently from those attached to the world of business and Newtonian science and yet are close enough in cultural and historical experience so that we might learn something from them — something immediately useful?

They are the artists among us.

TURNING FROM ARTFUL WORK TO JOBS

Science and art are two sides of the same coin. They are both attempts to craft a view of the world around us. All work is part science, part art.

We have come to think of art as pleasure, decoration, something to hang on our walls, to play on our stereo during a quiet dinner, to view on a movie screen, a respite from work. Art, for most of us, is not useful but pleasurable. Art is not something we do but something we enjoy.

However, pre-Newtonian, preindustrial people drew no basic distinction between art and utility. They appreciated a product as artful if it was well made. The product, or work of art, was for human use: a finely crafted sword, a well-built home, a cathedral, a chair, a manuscript. These "artifacts" embodied spiritual meaning. A sword emulated a crucifix. The outline of a home imitated the shape of a protective dragon.

What we now think of as decorative or pleasurable art, for example, painting and music, was also seen as utilitarian in the past. Its function was to instruct, inform, and illuminate the spiritual. Leonardo da Vinci wrote in his notebooks, "A good painter has two chief objects to paint — man and the intention of his soul" (Crosby, 1959, 327).

In other words, artists once made things for the spiritual and material use of people, and the test of the thing's excellence was the artist's success in making what was intended. Painter and art teacher Robert Henri wrote, "Art is . . . a result of a grip on the fundamentals of nature, the spirit of life, the constructive force, the secret of growth, a real understanding of the relative importance of things, order, balance" (1984, 226).

Pre-Newtonian people also did not draw a rigid distinction between art and work. Work well accomplished *was* art. Later, the scientific view became the prevailing perspective of industrial revolutionists, and it can be argued that science drove art out of work. Ananda Coomaraswamy was a curator at Boston's Museum of Fine Arts, a philosopher, art historian, and linguist. He published and spoke extensively about the history of art. He wrote, "We have come to think of art and work as incompatible, or at least independent categories, and have for the first time in history created an industry without art" (1956, 61).

How did we come to view work as something we perform in order to survive and art as merely something we suspend on our walls or perform at our leisure? Coomaraswamy believed that our society was the first in history to find it natural that some things are beautiful and others are useful. He saw that our ability to mass-produce goods left the individual artist at a distinct competitive disadvantage. Thus artists were robbed of their art and instead were forced to find "jobs." As they turned from art to jobs, a wedge severed artfulness from work.

The cultural process of changing from artful work to jobs resulted in at least two significant consequences: First, work came to be viewed as something one must do in order to survive and achieve, while art came to be viewed as pleasure. Second, the reward for work became extrinsic more than intrinsic. Instead of pursuing rewards in our work, we began to pursue them more in our leisure activities and in the external rewards that employers provide.

AN INTRODUCTION TO ARTFUL WORK

What exactly is "artful work"? How can artistic sensibilities be integrated into our perception of work and into our organizational work lives? The artist's perspective on work is:

- **All work can be artful**
- **The reward for artful work is in the doing**
- **The ambition of artful work is joy**
- **All work is spiritual work**
- **Artful work demands that the artist owns the work process**
- **Artful work requires consistent and conscious use of the self**
- **As the artist creates the work, the work creates the artist**

These are the beliefs of artful work. Together they form, like the beliefs of Newtonian science, a paradigm, a way of thinking and seeing. Artful work is a useful paradigm for human organizations because it is about work and human energy. The beliefs of artful work are drawn from the writings of artists about their work, from many dialogues with artists, and from my own experience as an artist.

These beliefs may seem to include unusual terms regarding work — art, joy, spirit, and use of the self. Management consultant Peter Block wrote, "Somebody save us from the language of institutions" (1993, 131). He reminded us that a new perspective often requires a new language.

PHYSICAL AND MENTAL APPROACHES

Newtonian science produced wonderful ideas, saved us much physical labor, provided comfort and ease, and created interesting toys. It has not, however, brought us closer to our interior lives or to the natural world in which we live. Thus we made it easier to wash the dishes and harder to find serenity. In the process we sold lots of dishwashers and detergent as well as psychotherapy and self-help books. In our workplaces in particular, we often behave as if we have no interior lives at all.

Newtonian science is also a dubious approach to running human organizations. We thought it was valid because we engaged in "management science" after the Second World War. This was a time when the only thing America had to do in order to make money was exist; the rest of the world's industrial base was in shambles. Thus the conclusions of management science suffer from what statisticians would call "sampling error" — making conclusions from unsound data.

Because Newtonian science focuses our attention on the external world and on our mental capacities, it encourages us to seek two kinds of approaches to our challenges: physical and mental. In the process we ignore other approaches, the emotional and spiritual approaches that are the lifeblood of artfulness.

Physical approaches include techniques such as restructuring organizations, revising organizational charts, or installing new equipment or processes. These approaches amount to moving things around, moving people around, acquiring new things or people, or getting rid of things or people. Such efforts please us for a time, much as rearranging the furniture in our home might please us.

Mental approaches relate to ideas — ideas about how organizations function or ought to function, ideas about quality and service, ideas about management. We develop or purchase these ideas then typically fail to make them work.

We entertain the hope, over and over, that physical and mental approaches alone will help us meet our challenges. They won't, because we are looking for solutions in the wrong places. We look only where our prevailing beliefs allow us to look, and our prevailing beliefs allow us only to look at physical and mental approaches, at techniques and ideas.

SEEKING THE UMBRELLA

Looking for solutions in the wrong places is like "seeking the umbrella." When I pull into my driveway in a downpour and need my umbrella to avoid getting drenched, the umbrella, most likely, is in the house. Somewhere in the back of my mind I know it is in the house, yet I paw hopefully around the back seat of my car nonetheless. Likewise, when I am in the house and need to get to the car in a torrent, where is the umbrella? In the car, of course. Still I open closets, searching.

I do this fruitless searching because it momentarily relieves my sense of powerlessness. I do it also because I hope that things will be easier for me than they really are.

12

Tom Robbins, in his novel, *Skinny Legs and All*, described an example of "seeking the umbrella." The novel concerns the spiritual awakening of a young waitress named Ellen Cherry. In the final chapter, Robbins wrote:

> She understood suddenly, and for no particular reason of which she
> was aware, that it was futile to work for political solutions to
> humanity's problems because humanity's problems were not political.
> Political problems did exist, all right, but they were entirely secondary.
> (1991, 459)

Ellen Cherry's epiphany occurred because of her experience as a waitress in, of all things, an Arab-Israeli restaurant in Manhattan. Her job exposed her to the quagmire of the Middle East. Imagine her now as a secretary in a corporate headquarters. With a few changes, and perhaps apologies to Robbins, Ellen's words become:

> She understood suddenly, and for no particular reason of which she
> was aware, that it was futile to work for physical and mental solutions
> to organizational problems because organizational problems were nei-
> ther physical nor mental. Physical and mental problems did exist, all
> right, but they were entirely secondary.

If the solutions to the challenges of our organizations are not in the physical or mental domains, then where are they?

FOUR HUMAN ENERGIES

All organizations consist of people. We need to remember that fact because, although it is obvious, we often behave as if it were false. We forget that all organizational change and success rest on the energy of people. We are too often busy with techniques rather than with ourselves and the people around us.

Because all organizations consist of people, answers to the questions, Where are the primary challenges of today's organizations? or Where are the resources to meet those challenges? ought to derive from understanding what it means to be a person.

People incorporate four energies: physical, mental, emotional, and spiritual. This is only one system we might use to examine ourselves, but it is a fairly common one. It is found with slight variations in the work of personal-growth authors such as Steven Covey (1990) and Alice Mack (1992). We might also use the Eastern system of seven chakras. But how many centers of energy people incorporate and how we label them are not the point. The primary issue is that we now allow only certain forms of energy to permeate our workplaces and we devalue other forms.

Physical energy resides in tissue, muscle, organs, and cells. It is tangible and solid. It involves how and when we move our bodies, engage in work or play, or merely arrange physical objects. We expend physical energy when we move our bodies and replenish it during rest.

Mental energy occupies thoughts, ideas, evaluations, memories, and plans for the future. Like the body, the mind requires nourishment; its food is words or numbers served in a manner that stimulates and enlightens.

13

Its structure is logic and science. Mental energy is the fundamental energy of the scientific world view.

Emotional energy inhabits feelings such as the sorrow of loss, the joy of achievement, the shame of a scolded child, or the wonder of newness. Emotional energy is liquid; it flows like a broad river, at one moment turbulent and muddy, at the next serene and clear. It often rushes along beneath the surface of things, trying to break through whatever defensive crust we may manufacture to suppress it. Our current Newtonian perspective does not place much trust in emotional energy, and we do not trust it in the workplace.

Spiritual energy arises from our beliefs about the unseen forces that shape our reality and about our relationship to those forces. It concerns the divine, spirit, soul, and the relationships among them. Spiritual energy gives meaning to our lives and bonds us together in community. It is the source of our impulse to create and is significant to our work. It is anchored in our answers to unanswerable questions — questions about how the world works and in our beliefs about our place in the world.

These four sources of energy entwine to form a complex web of wholeness and interdependence. A healthy physical body promotes good feeling, increases mental capacity, and creates spiritual peace. An emotional upset will generate physical manifestations, confuse our thinking, and cause our spirit to plunge. The quality of our intellect influences physical, emotional, and spiritual well-being. Spirit is either nurtured or suffers as our feelings vacillate from hope to despair or our body supports or betrays us.

The process of bringing all of our energy together, of calling all of ourselves to a particular moment or task, is the process that results in artistry. It is called *centering* and forms the basis of the next chapter.

THINGS WE ARE TIRED OF HEARING ABOUT

I talked with a man who directs executive development programs for a large university business school. I wanted to discover what concepts executives in his programs were tired of hearing about.

"Are they tired of hearing about visions?" I asked.

"Yep! They are tired of hearing about visions."

"Values?"

"That one, too!"

"Empowerment?"

"Especially that one!"

"Paradigm shifts?"

"Gag!"

Why do we tire of hearing about concepts that we initially embrace and imbue with so much hope? We welcome them but fail to translate them into viable realities, tire of our own failure, then blame the failure on the ideas themselves. It isn't the ideas we tire of, it is our own inability to translate them into viable realities.

The experience is like having company for the weekend. They arrive. It is good to see them. The visit begins with warm embraces. But now they are here for the whole weekend! Unless they are in some way important to us, we tire of them. We can't think of what to do and can't wait for them to leave. When they have left we blame them for our misery.

Why do we fail to translate our wonderful concepts into viable realities? Because we maintain them at the level of concepts. We invest them only with mental energy. We often skip the step of absorbing ideas into our emotional and spiritual selves. We may like the *idea* of having company for the weekend, but when they actually show up . . . well, that's a different matter — it's unsettling.

WHY BOTHER WITH ARTISTRY?

The issues we now believe to be important, issues such as values, empowerment, service, quality, and responsible care of our environment, are matters of feeling and spirit. We know these issues are crucial to organizational success and we have the technology to succeed. Still, it seems there are more stories about why our efforts fail than there are success stories.

We also know, occasionally clearly but often dimly, that some elusive ingredient in our work is missing — artistry. We can pledge ourselves to noble goals and lofty visions and embrace the technique of the moment. However, until we engage ourselves *artfully* with the work needed to achieve our goals and visions, our goals will remain unfulfilled and our techniques will fail us.

I am attempting in this book to point us toward a way of thinking about ourselves and our organizations which will help us bring more of the elusive missing ingredient — artistry — to our workplaces.

CENTERING

2

*I have come to feel that we live in
a universe of spirit, which materializes
and de-materializes grandly.*

The concept of centering is fundamental to understanding artful work. Centering, as I use the term, comes from the writing of poet and potter M. C. Richards (to whom I am not related), who described it as an act that occurs both on the potter's wheel and within the potter. In the following quote, the author, Deng Ming-Dao, describes the physical process of centering a lump of clay, which eventually becomes a vase, pitcher, bowl, or cup.

When a potter begins to throw a pot, she picks up a lump of clay, shapes it into a rough sphere, and throws it onto the spinning potter's wheel. It may land off-center, and she must carefully begin to shape it until it is a smooth cylinder. Then she works the clay, stretching and compressing it as it turns. First it is a tower, then it is like a squat mushroom. Only after bringing it up and down several times does she slowly squeeze the revolving clay until its walls rise from the wheel. She cannot go on too long, for the clay will begin to "tire" and then sag. She gives it the form she imagines, then sets it aside. (1992, 12)

There is, however, much more than a physical process involved. Centering is not mere technique. Richards wrote:

When we act out of an inner unity, when all of ourselves is present in what we do, then we can be said to be "on center." Part of our skill as potters is to use all the clay on the wheel in any given form. Our wholeness as persons is expressed in using all of ourselves in any given act. In this way the self integrates its capacities into a personal potency, as a being who serves life from his center at every instant. (1989, 36)

THE EMOTIONAL UNDERCURRENT

We are "on center" when our entire self is present in what we do, including our emotional self. Emotion drives many events that occur in our organizational lives. But expressing emotion is generally absent. We often pretend emotion doesn't exist and squander its potency.

Potency. It means having power, being persuasive, effective, or strong. It also means developing potential. There is potency in emotion; but because we do not trust emotion, because our perspective encourages us to mistrust it, we lose its potency.

For example, a group of senior managers meets to evaluate and rank their subordinates. The result of the meeting will determine who gets promoted and who doesn't and who gets what kind of raise. If a rumored downsizing occurs, the people at the bottom of the ranking will be asked to leave the company. These are consequential matters. The lives of many people will be altered.

19

I am observing from the back of the room. I notice a lack of emotion among the participants in this meeting. They are treating their drill as a gardener might search through a patch of ground, dispassionately pulling weeds. One of the managers leaves his seat, moves to the back of the room, and sits next to me.

"This is awful, isn't it?" he whispers.

I agree. It is awful.

"They are talking about one of my guys right now," he says. "He's what we call a 'weak sister.' A nice guy, really, and a solid performer. Not spectacular but solid. He ticked off the guy who's talking right now, trying to tear him down. My guy was right, but it doesn't matter."

So the speaker is angry, but he doesn't say he is angry. Instead he mechanically dredges for details to prove that the man being evaluated deserves a low ranking. The man next to me is disgusted by the whole affair, but he doesn't say it. Instead he calmly refutes the argument being presented. All of the energy of the participants is not present. Potency has vanished.

I wonder what would happen if the speaker said, "I'm just ticked off at this guy"? I wonder what would happen if the man next to me said, "This whole process feels awful"?

Another example: A team meets to make decisions about launching a new product. One woman, who has more experience in such matters than anyone else in the room, offers several suggestions. Nobody responds to her ideas. In fact nobody responds to anyone else's ideas. Everyone argues for his or her own ideas. They are all frustrated and the discussion goes nowhere.

20

Most of what they are saying begins with the words, "Yeah, but . . .", as each person gives cursory acknowledgment to what another has said, then goes off on his or her own tangent. Soon everyone is feeling powerless and incapable of making the necessary decisions.

I wonder what would happen if the woman with all the right ideas said, "This is frustrating. Nobody is listening to anyone else"?

Later, I ask her why she didn't say something like that.

"I'd be accused of being too emotional. Emotions don't count around here."

Again, potency, the power to develop the potential of the moment, has vanished.

If the speaker in the first example said, "I'm just ticked off at this guy," and if the others in the room valued emotional energy, they would have the opportunity to change a situation they all hated. If the woman in the second example said, "This is frustrating. Nobody is listening to anyone else," and if the others in the room valued emotional energy, they would have the opportunity to change a situation that frustrated all of them.

They squandered their opportunities because expressing emotion isn't valued in their workplaces and because emotion frightens them — and most of us — in the meeting rooms of many of our companies.

In almost every office, conference room, and factory, in almost every organization, we have created a vast emotional undercurrent, a world of unexpressed, unaddressed feeling. This teeming abundance of feeling influences every decision, every action, and every interchange among people. While we appear on the surface to be logical, objective, and rational, the forces of the emotional undercurrent are at play: fear, anger, passion, shame, guilt, disgust, joy, frustration, caring, love, and loathing.

21

We cannot overestimate the importance of this emotional undercurrent. Unless a person is in deep denial or has so suppressed emotions that they are unreachable, he or she knows that this undercurrent is active. When we invest in pretending it does not exist, we lose twice; we lose the wasted energy of maintaining the pretense, and we lose the energy inherently contained in emotion.

THE FEELING CHECK

Avoiding emotional expression is the norm in the business universe, but there are exceptions. Some groups of people do respect the emotional undercurrent and have learned to shine light upon it. These are people who have given themselves permission to say things like, "I'm frustrated" or "I'm angry." They have learned to articulate their feelings and to use their emotional energy as a catalyst for transforming unproductive moments into productive ones. It is a struggle to learn such things and difficult to shed old pretenses, but it can be done.

Here is one example: Ten managers meet in a conference room at a San Francisco hotel. They are the senior managers of a division at a large financial services company. They are meeting to revisit and renew their organization's sense of purpose and to create a theme or program to galvanize and propel the organization. They are unused to this kind of endeavor. Until now each managed his or her own department, a single manager managed all of them, and that was that.

Their manager believes that the business would be better served by true partnerships among the people present. She called this meeting to begin forging those partnerships. Her name is Donna.

Although the managers know one another well, know Donna, and know what she intends, the initial hour of the meeting is strained and tense. There is little dialogue among them. They direct their comments only to Donna.

Then Donna asks the group to engage in what she terms a "feeling check."

"I'd like to hear from each of you what you are feeling about this meeting so far," she says.

The replies are:

"Uncomfortable."

"Nervous."

"Wary."

"Disbelieving."

"Frustrated."

And so forth.

"Can we spend some time away from the agenda talking about why we feel the way we do?" Donna asks. She suspects that until the feelings are brought to the table, their work together will be impeded.

They discuss their doubts that Donna will really let go of the reins; they are afraid she will not be able to give up control. A few raise a contrary fear that she might successfully let go of the reins, forcing them to assume increased levels of responsibility. They worry that they may not be up to the challenge. The managers also talk about unsuccessful past attempts to work collaboratively as well as some lingering mistrust of one another. They struggle for solutions.

Finally the group develops agreements with Donna about how to handle situations during the times when she seems to be holding on too tightly or when they want more direction from her. They also make agreements about how to handle instances when they feel mistrustful of one another.

After they complete the agreements, the group experiences a heightened level of energy and excitement. They are ready to move forward. They have surmounted the barrier of anxious, fearful energy and created new emotional space for enjoyment. The meeting proceeds. Although they had scheduled two days to complete their agenda, they are surprised to find that they have finished after only one. The team agreed to a new organizational theme and together created a plan to implement it.

THE SPIRITUAL UNDERCURRENT

Alongside the emotional undercurrent is a spiritual one. Its workings are every bit as profound and powerful as those related to the emotional undercurrent.

A product manager once told me, "I just can't get excited about selling these damned pizza sticks. They are vastly overpriced and have zero nutritional value. I won't let my kids eat them. So I am going through the motions, doing the best I can, and hoping this job doesn't last much longer."

This man's spirit was suffering. He was engaged in work that had no meaning to him. He was doing his job but without the fullness of his energy. He lost, his company lost, we all lost.

24

Another man, the new president of a chemical company, was creating a video to communicate his hopes about the future of the organization. The woman hired to make the video told me, "I have been trying for a month to understand what he wants to say. He has a vision somewhere buried inside him, but it is buried so deeply he can't find it."

The man and I spoke at length about his vision and his hopes. He told me about the products the company offered, its strategy, acquisitions he was considering, and how he wanted to expand the business into different countries. He told me about everything except himself.

I asked him, "Why do you want to run a chemical company?"

"It isn't about running a chemical company," he replied quickly, startled that the conversation had switched focus. There was a long pause. He looked away, his gaze fixed far outside the big window in his office.

He said, "I imagine a huge organism that has three parts: this company, my country, and the people who work here. The three parts of this organism feed one another, nurture one another. The organism flourishes because all the parts help one another.

"I am a chemical engineer by training," he said, "but that isn't why I run a chemical company. I do it because I want to help that organism thrive."

Bingo!

The video turned out to be sensational and won a prestigious award.

This man's sense of purpose is not all that surprising. What is surprising, and sad, is the difficulty many people have in articulating these affinities and the embarrassment they feel when their deepest desires come to light.

Later he said, "I was reluctant to talk about why I do what I do because I thought it might sound sappy."

We lose the potency of our spiritual energy when we think we sound "sappy," when we work at jobs that do not engage our spirit, or when we ourselves deny or suppress that spirit.

USING THE MATERIALS OF THE MOMENT

M. C. Richards also wrote:

> Every person is a special kind of artist and every activity is a special art. An artist creates out of the materials of the moment, never again to be duplicated. This is true of the painter, the musician, the dancer, the actor; the teacher; the scientist; the businessman; the farmer — it is true of us all, whatever our work, that we are artists so long as we are alive to the concreteness of a moment and do not use it to some other purpose. (1989, 40)

Every person is an artist and every activity is a special art. Evaluating the performance of others is an art. Managing is an art. Carpentry, marketing, research, and distributing products are all arts. Making decisions is an art. Being effective in a meeting, or as part of a team, is an art.

Our work is artful when we, like the potter at her wheel, are "alive to the concreteness of a moment" and "create out of the materials of the moment." Being alive to the concreteness of the moment means being fully attentive to all that is happening in the present.

The materials of the moment are more than the physical things in front of us — more than simply the clay, a report from a task force, a page of numbers, a set of charts, a machine, or ideas written on a white board. The materials of the moment include emotion and spirit. When we include them, we become who we truly are and bring all of ourselves to our work. We become centered *and* artful.

ALL WORK CAN BE ARTFUL

3

*Every person is a special kind of artist
and every activity is a special art.*

Norman Maclean, best known as the author of *A River Runs Through It*, wrote, "A lot of questions about the woods can't be answered by staying all the time in the woods. . . ." (1992, 104). In the next few chapters we will leave the woods of work and organizations as we now know them. When we return to whatever patch of the woods is familiar to us, I hope we will have new ways of seeing our current challenges.

We will enter the woods inhabited by artists. Poets, potters, writers, filmmakers, and other artists hold strikingly similar beliefs about how the world works. These beliefs are significant for us and our organizations because they are about human energy and work.

The time is right to explore artful work and its implications for business. Others are also exploring this terrain: Max DePree wrote *Leadership Is an Art* (1989) and *Leadership Jazz* (1992), James Autry introduced us to the poetry of business in *Love and Profit* (1991), and Peter Vaill wrote *Managing as a Performing Art* (1989). The link between art and work is already forged.

The threads we are currently weaving into our understanding of work and business, threads such as empowerment, ownership, and vision, are consistent with the beliefs of artists. The perspective of artists can be a powerful guide as we reinvent organizations and rethink work.

Chapters 3 through 8 describe artful work, the set of beliefs that form the world view of the artist. Artful work is a way of thinking about ourselves as workers. The beliefs were already introduced and are restated here as a road map to what follows.

- **All work can be artful**
- **The reward for artful work is in the doing**
- **The ambition of artful work is joy**
- **All work is spiritual work**
- **Artful work demands that the artist owns the work process**
- **Artful work requires consistent and conscious use of the self**
- **As the artist creates the work, the work creates the artist**

BILLY AND MY BONNEVILLE

In the early 1970s I bought a venerable and well-used 1958 Pontiac Bonneville. It was a faded brown, with a beige interior kept spotless by clear plastic covers. The car was confidently approaching 120,000 miles. It reminded me of an aircraft carrier. I often imagined a scaled-down helicopter, about the size of a wild rabbit, landing on its enormous broad, flat trunk. It didn't cost much. It needed only a new set of tires.

I wasn't interested in spending much money on the old boat, so I took it to a place that sold retread tires. That was where I saw Billy at work. Billy was in his mid-twenties, small, thin, and gregarious; and could Billy ever change tires! I maneuvered the car onto Billy's lift. He went to his workbench and started a timer. Then he attacked the car with frenzy and grace. Billy was truly balletic around the car, removing the old wheels, changing the tires, balancing the new ones, and replacing the wheels on the car. Billy was the Nureyev of tire changers.

At the instant the car returned to the grimy shop floor, Billy tapped the timer again. He looked at the timer, then turned to me with an expression of pure joy on his face.

"A new record," he shouted. "Damn, a new record!"

Billy's coworkers applauded.

Billy held the first belief of artful work: *all work can be artful*.

FOUR QUESTIONS ABOUT ARTFULNESS

Many of us are at best ambivalent and at worst destructive toward the artist in ourselves. We identify our artistic selves with art itself and devalue both.

We might encourage the artist in a child, but we too often ensure the child learns that a career as an artist is impractical. "Art is okay as a hobby," we say, "but when you go to school, study something useful."

We become adults who believe that art and work are mutually exclusive. The net result is that we often fail to develop our capacity for artful work. We create emotional distance with regard to work rather than engagement. The net result for companies is a dangerous lack of the very inventiveness, flexibility, and courage they so sorely need.

There are questions we can ask ourselves to determine whether we might do any particular work artfully.

- **Do I care about the work itself?**
- **Can I express myself through the work?**
- **Am I committed to the meaning of the work?**
- **Am I tenacious enough to do the work well?**

DO I CARE ABOUT THE WORK ITSELF?

My neighbor mows his woods! Once or twice each year he propels a dilapidated, gasoline-driven lawn mower through the acre and a half of trees surrounding his house, chopping down small plants, trees, and weeds, grinding up twigs, sending up smoke signals of exhaust, creating a manicured forest. Sometimes he will stop for a moment or two to chat, and I marvel at how much he seems to be enjoying himself. He never stops for long but is eager to get back to his mower. His house in the woods is a weekend retreat from a townhouse in the city.

He once told me, "I like mowing, but I don't have a lawn back home."

My woods, on the other hand, are a jumble of fallen trees, a mishmash of plant life. I want to tell him, "This is the woods. There are supposed to be twigs, plants, and weeds on the ground!" But I must admit his woods do look nice in a sanitized way, and I wouldn't mind if my woods looked like his. I rationalize that I don't mow my woods for obscure ecological reasons, but the truth is I don't mow my woods because I don't care that much about manicuring forests, and I hate pushing a lawn mower. I don't do it for the same reason I mulch most of the open property around my house. I simply cannot commit to gardening.

Psychologist Rollo May wrote that art requires engagement. May reported that W. H. Auden once said, "The poet marries the language, and out of this marriage the poem is born" (1975, 97). Today, when we talk of being married to work, we are often talking of workaholism, but Auden meant something quite different. He meant that the poem emanates from the poet's engagement with language.

A painter engages with the landscape. A musician engages with the melody. An actor engages with the character. Billy engages with tire changing. My neighbor engages with mowing. I doubt I will ever mow my woods or become an artful gardener because I do not or cannot engage with the work involved.

Engaging means choosing to involve oneself in or commit oneself to something. Engagement occurs when we experience a deep sense of caring about the work, a sense that what we are doing is worthwhile in and of itself.

I once worked as part of a team created to direct an organizational

31

change project. Two companies had merged. The leaders of the newly formed company recognized that each of the former companies had different strengths. They wanted to be careful that the culture of the new company embraced the strengths of both former companies. Other members of the team were employees of the former companies. I felt passionate about this project. It was an opportunity to do a merger the right way and to create a corporate culture that served everyone.

Over spaghetti and Chianti, another member of the team said to me, "I figured out what bothers me about you."

I was startled and curious. I didn't know until that moment that anything about me bothered him.

"What is it?" I asked, self-consciously twirling my spaghetti.

"You are a fanatic," he said. "You are just very fanatical about this project."

Now I was really curious. I twirled faster. Was he telling me that he was bothered by me because I cared more about his company than he did, that I was more engaged in his company's success than he wanted to be?

I asked him if that was true.

"Sure," he replied, "let's face it. I'll do my job, but I'm not going to get too wrapped up in it, and I'm not going to put too much energy into it. It's just my job, after all."

What he meant was that he was not going to engage with the work. He had chosen to approach his work in a way that precluded the possibility for him to be artful.

"Why are you involved in this project?" I asked.

"My boss thought it would be good experience for me. You don't say no to him."

He was unable or unwilling to engage with the work because he did not care about it. He cared mostly about not displeasing his boss.

To engage also means to choose. We frequently forget that we have choices. My dinner partner might have chosen to engage with the work. If that choice was unappealing, he might have chosen to risk telling his boss that his commitment to the project was low and that he could not engage with the work necessary to make the project a success. He made a third choice — compliance. Compliance produces artlessness.

CAN I EXPRESS MYSELF THROUGH THE WORK?

Actors in rehearsal speak of "going off book," or reciting one's lines without the script. Before going off book the actor is guided by the script, trying to find the character in the words and directions on a printed page. Like the man who didn't want to displease his boss, the actor is using an external guide. Going off book means that the actor is no longer looking to an external source — the script — for guidance. This is not merely a matter of having memorized the lines. An actor who goes off book finds self-expression through the character. The actor stops wondering how to be, takes ownership of the character, and becomes self-expressive.

The stereotypical dehumanizing assembly line is a striking example of work that does not go off book. Everything is driven by "the line." The line provides the script. There is little room for self-expression except sabotage.

In much other organizational work, we avoid the moment of going off

33

book. "The line" is less visible perhaps, but it is only questionably less dehumanizing. This is "the corporate line," what we are supposed to think and how we are supposed to be. It is a more subtle kind of line but a line nonetheless — a line that blocks self-expression.

34

Going off book is an uncomfortable and demanding process requiring the actor to be authentic, inhabit the character and the play, and artfully create its structure through interacting with other actors and with props, all at the same time. Most of us have more practice seeking external guidance, looking for the "right" way to work, expressing only what someone else wants to hear. Sometimes, also, the penalty, or at least the perceived penalty, for going off book seems too harsh. We imagine dire consequences: the anger of a boss or coworker, the loss of a promotion or job. When the penalty seems too harsh, we withdraw from ourselves and from artistry.

Self-expression, in the artistic sense, does not mean expressing one's personality, the visible aspect of the self. Rather, it means expressing one's self as a person — physically, mentally, emotionally, and spiritually. It means calling forth and giving voice to those aspects of the self that are not immediately apparent: an idea, a feeling, a spiritual longing, or a belief. Self-expression is unselfconscious. It is as natural as an unpracticed gesture but not easy when we are concerned with who we are *supposed* to be rather than who we *are*.

AM I COMMITTED TO THE MEANING OF THE WORK?

All work creates something. Artfulness demands that we engage with the process of the work and with its product. The meaning of the work resides in the meaning of what we create. Laurence Boldt, an author and career consultant, wrote, "Your life's work is your way of making this world a better place" (1993, 15). We have a chance to work artfully when we believe that what our work creates makes the world a better place.

A friend once worked for a consumer products company that prided itself on creating quality products that made life easier. The company manufactured microwaves, food processors, and other appliances. When it began making weaponry, he told me that many people in the company were shocked and disappointed. He refused a promotion that would have transferred him into the weapons division because he could not commit to the product.

Engaging with a product requires that we ask a question of our spirit: What does the product mean? Instead, we usually ask, What is it for? Or, perhaps, How does it work? We tend to ask questions of utility, not meaning.

Robert Henri expressed very simply an artist's wish for engagement with his or her product: "I would like you to go to your work with a consciousness that it is more important than anything else you might do" (1984, 177).

AM I TENACIOUS ENOUGH TO DO THE WORK WELL?

Donald Hall, author and literary critic, reported that he once asked the famous sculptor, Henry Moore, "Now that you are eighty, you must know the secret of life. What is the secret of life?" Moore replied:

> The secret of life is to have a task, something you do your entire life, something you bring everything to, every minute of the day for your

whole life. And the most important thing is — it must be something you cannot possibly do! (1993, 54)

Now that's tenacity!

Hall stated that Moore's task was to be the greatest sculptor who ever lived and to know it.

If we are to be artful, we must dedicate ourselves in such a way that we struggle through uncertainty, suffer pain, attempt to learn everything there is to know about our craft, and practice, practice, practice.

All work can be artful, but the artfulness lies in our approach to the work and not in the work itself. These four questions — of caring about the work itself, of whether the work provides opportunity for self-expression, of our commitment to meaning, and of our own tenacity — form a kind of litmus test for our ability to work artfully at the type of work we choose.

36

WORK, REWARDS, AND JOY

4

*But surely nothing can be said to work
that stands between a man
and the fullness of his being.*

The second and third beliefs of artful work are closely related. They are: *the reward for artful work is in the doing,* and *the ambition of artful work is joy.* Joy is the ultimate reward for artful work. It is joy the artist seeks, the reason for the artist's willingness to persist through whatever troubles lie along the path to artistry.

JOY

What is joy? Psychologist Mihaly Csikszentmihalyi has studied times when people reported feeling enjoyment. He wrote:

Enjoyable events occur when a person has not only met some prior expectation or satisfied a need or a desire but also gone beyond what he or she has been programmed to do and achieved something unexpected, perhaps even something unimagined before. (1990, 46)

38

Joy arrives on the wings of discovery and surprise. It inhabits us when we excel. Joy is not a goal of artful work but the result of doing something challenging and doing it well — so well that the doing leads us into realms we did not expect. We surprise ourselves. Joy occurs when we transcend who we think we are and what we think we are capable of creating.

We tend to see work as a perpetual sequence of problems to solve rather than as the pursuit of joy. Perhaps, given our immense need to solve problems to prove that we are good workers, we subconsciously create problems so we will have "work" to do.

On a Friday afternoon, weary of having so many problems to solve, too many of us "dis-solve" into alcohol, parties we don't care about, people we would rather not be with, or to the boat we secretly view as a hole in the water, into which we throw money.

In the words of Laurence Boldt, "As long as we view work as a means of solving problems, we 'live for the weekends' . . . from a problem-solving approach, escape is what passes for joy" (1993, 7).

The degree to which we seek joy within our work is the degree to which we invite artfulness. We deserve joy, every one of us, but we don't expect or seek joy in our work when we believe the reward for work lies in approval, external rewards, and celebrations.

MYSTIFICATION AND THE NEED FOR APPROVAL

I coauthored a set of materials, including a questionnaire intended to assess the quality of a team's work together (1994). My coauthor and I used the questionnaire with many teams in order to validate it and provide normative data. We also called friends and clients who were, for the most part, eager to help. We offered to provide the assessment material at no cost, in exchange for the data resulting from the team's self-assessment.

One friend, who worked for a large company, agreed to assess several teams. She later reneged on her agreement, saying, "I'd like to help. I'd enjoy doing it, and it would be good for everybody concerned, but there are no rewards in this organization for doing this kind of thing. So I let it slide."

Her attitude toward rewards is pervasive and represents our confusion about the notion that the purpose of artistic work is joy. Joy is an internal reward; we give it to ourselves. My friend was unwilling to do what she believed was right and what would have given her joy because she wanted approval.

Our culturally induced need for approval is tremendous. The current paradigm requires it and much advertising encourages it. We are inundated with messages telling us how to gain approval — wear Italian suits, use a deodorant especially and precisely formulated for your needs, eat the right breakfast cereal, order the right aperitif or the right soft drink, drive the right car. Don't think about what you want; think about what will gain approval.

From the moment we enter a classroom, and probably before that, we are immersed in a universe in which someone else judges and either approves or disapproves of our work. By the time we join the working world, most of us are well trained; we believe approval is everything. Our artfulness has already been squelched.

A distraught friend told me that her son quit high school because he concluded that high school trained him, first and foremost, for organizational life. This teenager's appraisal of high school and organizational life was, "Sit still and wait to be called on. Live by the clock. Let someone else decide if you are good or not. Don't go outside unless it's for play; important things only happen indoors." Without judging the young man's decision, I think his formulation seems a respectable analysis.

John Bradshaw's *Creating Love* is primarily about love and relationships, but striking parallels about how we treat our work and ourselves as workers nestle within his ideas. Bradshaw's notion of "mystification" is particularly relevant. He wrote that mystification is

> an altered state of consciousness in which a person feels and believes
> that there is something wrong with them as they are. The person then
> creates a false self in order to be accepted by their parents or other
> crucial survival figures. (1994, 7)

Bradshaw also stated, "Once we come to believe that we are this false self, we do not know that we do not know who we are" (1994, 7). When we are mystified, we bring our false, mystified selves to work with us, and our organizations reflect our mystification. In our sense of self as workers, we do not know that we do not know who we are as workers. We conduct much of our work while mystified, and we often create artless organizations that perpetuate our blindness to ourselves.

Most of us bear huge barriers to seeing our own mystification.

Bradshaw listed some of those barriers. For example, we gave up our wills in conformity to patriarchal rules; we have become numb and no longer know what we feel; we do not trust our own ideas; we learned never to question the rules. These barriers preclude artfulness.

A man who works for a large insurance company is an example of a mystified person. We were sitting in a courtyard on a sunny summer day. He was talking about the trauma of having recently uprooted his family as a result of accepting a job transfer that he truly did not want but was afraid to refuse. He said that he was unable to sleep, and when he did sleep he was plagued by nightmares.

As we spoke it became clear to him that his fear of refusing the transfer was a vestige of his need to please his father. This pattern of fear had troubled him for all of his thirty-five years. In other words, his career decisions up until that point were largely a product of his mystification. He did not enjoy his work; he enjoyed only the approval he received from his superiors.

Bradshaw wrote that we are culturally mystified by patriarchy. A patriarchy is dominated by male power, although the cultural standards may be enforced by women as well. According to Bradshaw, among the most damaging standards are blind obedience, repression of all emotions except fear, destruction of individual willpower, and repression of thinking whenever it departs from authority (1994, 26).

Writing about love, Bradshaw traced our mystification to our parents' patriarchal upbringing:

My parents and relatives learned that love was based on power, control, secrecy, shame, repression of emotions, and conformity of one's will to the will of another and of one's thoughts to the thoughts of another. (1994, 27)

Please reread that quotation, substituting the word "work" for the word "love." It carries the ring of truth, doesn't it?

Mystification is a source of denial that emotion and spirit contain any relevance for our work. We are legitimately mystified, most of us — confused between what we really want and what will gain approval.

In our culture, based on Newtonian science and supported by mystification, we typically gain the approval we desire by not being ourselves, by not being artful. At work, to the extent that people are rewarded for being other than themselves, the company contributes to sustaining mystification and the wish for approval. This process precludes the possibility of artful work because artistry requires engagement of the self — the true self, not the mystified self.

Our management technology, emerging as it does from the very paradigm it proposes to change, instead feeds the need for approval by focusing on reward systems, management style, recognition, and appraisal. This amounts to asking, How can we get people to do what we want them to do? The answer is, Encourage the need for approval. The implication is that, left to their own devices and free of the need for approval, people will do something destructive to the organization.

EXTERNAL REWARDS

External rewards, along with approval, provide another substitute for joy. It seems quite probable, as we continue to question our current practices, that most systems of performance appraisal, reward and recognition, and pay scales based on organizational hierarchy will be unmasked as detrimental to the human spirit. When these systems are used as instruments of coercion, they become the primary buttresses of the prevailing paradigm in organizations. Management consultant Peter Block wrote:

> Everyone likes the idea of pay for performance, but most of us have
> rarely experienced it. We most often get paid on the basis of how our
> boss evaluates us. This is more accurately called "pay for compliance."
> (1993, 172)

At their core, coercive systems that reward compliance reflect a demeaning view of humanity — that people ought to be, can be, manipulated to do someone else's will and still retain their humanness. So long as people accept that view of themselves, the systems function — marginally. Workers seek the literal or figurative pat on the back, managers and executives give them out, and everybody goes home a little satisfied, for a while. Artfulness and commitment suffer.

Psychologist Alfie Kohn (1993) said that rewards work only in situations in which the task being rewarded is essentially mindless. Even in those situations rewards might be detrimental because they entomb the initiative that could lead a worker to reinvent or find enjoyment in a mindless task.

Kohn wrote that whenever we say to someone, "Do this and you'll get that," we are attempting to control their behavior. In the process the person's interest in the "this" diminishes. Psychologist John Condry, who conducted a survey of research on the effects of rewards, found that people who are offered rewards tend to do the following:

Choose easier tasks, are less efficient in using the information available to solve novel problems, and tend to be answer oriented and more illogical in their problem-solving strategies. They seem to work harder and produce more activity, but the activity is of a lower quality, contains more errors, and is more stereotyped and less creative than the work of comparable nonrewarded subjects working on the same problems. (1977, 471–72)

Sounds like bad news.

Art demands willingness rather than compliance. Coomaraswamy stated:

The artist is normally either his own patron, deciding what is to be made, or formally and freely consents to the will of the patron, which becomes his own as soon as the commission has been accepted, after which the artist is only concerned with the good of the work to be done. (1956, 24)

To the extent a worker is willing or has taken on the will of the boss, the organization, or the customer, his or her work can be artful. The artist's doing is *willing* doing. The external rewards that preclude artfulness are used as instruments to gain compliance when the person is not truly willing to do the work itself.

CELEBRATIONS

The need for approval and the chase for external rewards are both used as substitutes for joyful work; so is celebration. I once consulted with a British company and was offended by the common attitude contained in the words,

"We don't want to hear any American 'rah-rah' stuff. Please leave the Tom Peters motivational tapes at home." In truth I am a very introverted person — so introverted that I sometimes watch other people fish. The "rah-rah" stuff is okay, but I am not particularly attracted to it. Except for those rare occasions when my beloved Philadelphia Phillies are in the pennant race, I am usually on the edge of the cheering crowd, not at its center. I don't even own any Tom Peters tapes. So why was I offended?

45

Neither the British nor the citizens of any other Western nation are better at finding joy in artful work than are Americans. However, my clients were, in a way, right about the "rah-rah" stuff. Although the attitude offended me at the time, I heard it often enough that I began wondering what truth it might contain. I arrived at this conclusion: Celebration is a wonderful thing, and I am very much in favor of it. However, celebration is not intrinsic to work; it is a pause in work. If the work contains no possibility for joy, if workers are so numb to their own experience that they don't miss joy, or if they expect only joyless work, they will need a slew of celebrations. When this occurs, as it often does, celebration is merely escape.

We will not gain anything if we simply curtail our efforts to manipulate people with rewards and eradicate gratuitous celebration. We will not gain anything unless we also work at resolving a fundamental failure of our organizations — the failure to match people with work that gives them joy. The amount of external rewards and celebrations needed to stimulate organizational performance is a measure of the depth of this failure, of the potential for artless work, and of the continuing mystification about who we truly are as workers.

THE SPAGHETTI METHOD OF
ORGANIZATIONAL REDESIGN

One statement above begs for more discussion: "a fundamental failure of our organizations — the failure to match people with work that gives them joy." It is possible to end this failure and to organize work in such a way that the potential for joy in work supplants approval, external rewards, and escapist celebration.

Susan was the director of a human service agency in trouble. Her organization provided both medical and counseling services. The agency's staff included six nurses, six counselors, three records assistants, and two receptionists. But Susan's funding was shrinking.

She believed her most valued employees were those who helped the agency's clients to grow in their personal lives. She also believed that those employees who most helped clients grow were those who were themselves growing and who most enjoyed their work. She knew she could not afford to keep those valued employees for too long. If they were growing, they would also want increasingly more challenging opportunities. The situation is similar to corporations that now recognize they can no longer offer "lifetime employment."

Susan said, "I'd be suspicious of anyone who wanted to be here for more than four or five years. If they did, they wouldn't be growing. If they weren't growing, how could they help anyone else grow? They would stop enjoying themselves and their work would suffer because I couldn't provide the challenges or bribe them to stay by offering more money, even if I wanted to."

46

She relinquished the idea that her agency could provide "long-term employment." She focused instead on "long-term employability" for her people. First, she asked each employee to create a statement that included answers to these questions:

- **What are your personal long-term goals?**

- **How does your employment here contribute to your goals?**

- **What might you do differently here so that you would enjoy your work and contribute more significantly to your goals?**

- **What kind of training do you need in order to do what you might do differently here?**

- **How does what you might do differently contribute to the agency's mission and meet our clients' needs?**

Susan met with each person to discuss his or her statement. She then held a meeting of all employees. She began by saying, "As of this moment there are no jobs here, but all of you are employed here. In this meeting we will reinvent everybody's job. As we do this we will ensure that we are faithful to the agency's mission, our clients' needs, and our own individual goals. Each of us will declare what work would give us the most enjoyment and growth. We will describe how the changes we want to make in our own work will benefit our clients and how those changes fit our mission." She also committed to provide training, within the limits of her resources.

The group created lists on large paper of what they needed to do to fulfill the agency's mission, what they now did, what they wanted to do, and what they felt their clients needed. They cut the lists into strips, one item per strip.

Then they sat in a circle surrounding a pile of paper strips. Someone remarked that the pile looked like some weird kind of spaghetti. Susan said, "Let us begin picking up the strips. Pick up the strips you want."

Thus was Susan's agency redesigned — with concern for joy and growth, clients' needs, empowered choice, and organizational mission. One counselor became a licensed psychologist. A records assistant trained to become a counselor. A nurse learned supervision. Susan did research about the effects of her approach on the agency's clients. Her research confirmed the effectiveness of the approach.

COMMITMENT OR COMPLIANCE

What we achieve by seeking approval, rewards, and celebrations, rather than enjoyment, is not greater productivity, creativity, or commitment. What we achieve is compliance.

In today's business climate, when we ask an employee to commit to quality, to a set of values, or to a vision, we are often asking for something we do not know how to obtain from people who may not wish to give it. We are asking for commitment — a very different proposition from compliance.

Quality, values, visions, empowerment, and many other issues are, first and foremost, emotions, attitudes, and matters of the spirit. They are more than behaviors. Mere compliance will not do. Kohn wrote:

> Of course, it is possible to get people to do something. That is what
> rewards, punishments, and other instruments of control are all about.
> But the desire to do something, much less to do it well, simply cannot
> be imposed; in this sense, it is a mistake to talk about motivating other
> people. (1993, 181)

WHEN ON CENTER

The reward for work is in the work itself, in the artist's reward — joy. M. C. Richards has a poetic view of the joy of artistic work. She wrote of joy that results from centeredness:

> When on center, the self *feels* different: one feels warm, *on rayonne,* in
> touch, the power of life a substance like an air in which one lives and
> has one's being with all other things, drinking it in and giving it off, at
> the same time quiet and at rest within it. (1989, 56)

It sounds wonderful, doesn't it? Can we bring that flavor to organizational work? Is it possible? Let's hope so.

THE POKER GAME

5

*A person wants to do something of his own,
to feel his own being alive and unique.*

We are seated at a table, thoroughly engaged in a thoroughly male ritual: the Friday night penny-ante poker game. With me are my friend Zeke and his brother Will. Zeke teaches biology at the local high school. Will is a senior manager at a publishing firm. There are also two men I have never met before. Sam is a retired truck driver and appears content with himself. Frank is Sam's son-in-law, a working truck driver, who is definitely not content with himself. Frank is what we might call "wound up tight."

After the first few hands, during which we each introduce the group to our favorite poker variant, the talk turns, as it always does in male endeavors at intimacy, to work.

Frank begins. "This afternoon the company did one of its silly damn 'we're all a big happy family' meetings."

52

Sam, who retired from the same company Frank now works for, asks, "What was it like?"

Frank replies, "Aw, hell, you know the drill, Sam. A couple speeches, a couple awards, some balloons, some new posters, some cookies and coffee. Drivers and secretaries checking each other out. Same old bull. Don't mean nothin'."

Frank sounds bitter. He finds no joy in his work, no reward in his paycheck, and no satisfaction in the Friday afternoon celebratory escape his company provides.

Sam smiles and says, "I used to like those things."

I am wondering now, *What is the difference between these two men? One is at peace with himself; the other is angry at life.*

"Well, I'm no part of their damn family," Frank says. "I'm a teamster. That's the family that gives a damn about me."

Zeke and Will remain silent. They are committed to their work and don't want to do anything with their lives except what they are doing — and fly-fishing whenever they can. They are also unfailingly polite, upbeat, and averse to conflict. I suspect they will change the subject soon. I, however, am ready to ask questions. The danger in writing a book is that every experience seems to contain the elusive key to the next chapter.

"Do you enjoy driving?" I ask Frank.

"When I was eighteen, I loved it," he says. He sits upright, puts his cards facedown on the table, places two cupped hands in front of him, grasping an imaginary steering wheel. I think of John Wayne riding tall in the saddle.

53

Frank slumps back into his chair, allows his hands to fall on the table. A gesture of despair. He picks up his cards and says, "Then I got to be twenty-eight. Then I got married and had a couple kids. Then I got to be thirty-eight. Now? Here to Columbus. Columbus to here. Here to Columbus. Columbus to here. Pick up the paycheck. Wait for them to call again. Back to Columbus.

"I go by the book," he continues. "They give me the book — rules, rules, rules — I follow it."

He looks down, runs his index finger across the table, as if he is studying the rules, as if the rules are engraved in the pale blue Masonite tabletop in Zeke's kitchen.

"The guys in the suits break the rules all the time. Me? I follow the rules. What do I get for it? Here to Columbus. Columbus to here."

I think that Frank is talking about more than just the rules of the road. Most of us carry around a set of "rules of life." If we don't acknowledge them and question them, and if they don't serve us well, we blame the rules and everybody else instead of ourselves. The rules are merely a reflection of the paradigm. Working artfully requires questioning the rules, challenging the paradigm.

I win a hand. My first win tonight.

Scooping a modest pile of change toward me, I ask Sam, "Did you like driving?"

"Yeah," he says. "Not every minute, mind you. But for the most part I enjoyed it. I even liked skidding down Route 80 to Columbus in February. It was a challenge to get there on time, and safely."

"Do you miss it?" I ask.

"Nah! I'm still having a good time!"

Frank is not finished. "I don't like it, and I don't like the money. I don't like Route 80 in February anymore. I'm forty-two, driving a truck, two kids, not enough money. The guys who break the rules make all the money."

Zeke, always the pacifier, tries to console Frank. Zeke looks above his cards and says, "I know a guy who earns a quarter of a million a year. He's a big deal in a steel company. He's miserable, really unhappy. Hates his job, hates his boss, hates his wife and kids, drinks too much."

Zeke fails to mollify Frank. "I'll take his job," says Frank. "If you're gonna be miserable, you might as well be rich while you're doing it. I'd do his job for two or three years, then I'm outta here. Off to the Florida Keys."

Frank is trapped. Trapped in believing his work cannot contain joy. Trapped in believing that the reward for his work lies outside the work itself.

I ask Sam what he is doing with himself now that he is retired.

He chuckles. "Well, a few years before I retired I got interested in landscaping. I read everything I could find about it and fooled around a little on my own property. When I quit driving, I started working on my place seriously. An acre and a half. When I finished, I liked it a lot but felt like tearing it out and starting all over again. I missed doing it. My wife wasn't crazy about that idea, so I started up a small landscaping business. It was just the neighbors at first, then they told other people. It keeps me interested. I like it."

Sam pauses. We are all looking at him: me, Zeke, Will, and Frank. We forget about our cards momentarily.

Then Sam tells us, "Maybe it isn't about money. Maybe enjoying your life is the real deal."

I smile in Sam's direction, but he is concentrating now on his cards. I am beginning to like Sam.

I think about "all work can be artful" and about "the reward for artistic work is in the doing." I think the work can be anything: changing tires, driving a truck, landscape gardening, managing, marketing, distributing products, accounting, writing reports and proposals, creating strategic plans, anything. I consider saying something about my thoughts but decide to remain silent. This is, after all, a poker game, not a seminar.

ALL WORK IS SPIRITUAL WORK

6

*Many forces are at work
besides our own devotion.
A mystery is at work.*

The fourth belief of artful work is: *all work is spiritual work.* All work has meaning beyond the surface realities of a job, a production schedule, a product, or a paycheck. All work concerns spirit and soul and involves our ability to connect them with surface realities.

"WE MUST DO IT FOR OUR SOULS"

Colleen is marketing manager for a company that creates and manufactures what it calls "furniture" for physically disabled children. The furniture consists of devices made of metal, wood, and nylon straps that enable physically disabled children to sit or stand in comfort.

The company enjoyed ten successful years before receiving news that a child had fallen out of one of its devices and suffered a fractured skull. The news was upsetting and caused much dismay to the workers, who prided themselves on the safety of their products.

The fall occurred in a classroom during a few minutes when there was no adult supervision. Another child had loosened the Velcro fasteners on the piece of furniture, causing the accident.

Much discussion and debate ensued within the company about this incident. While no one legally challenged the safety of the company's product, questions remained. Are we responsible? Could this happen again? What should we do?

Some believed the accident was a fluke and argued that the company had no responsibility, no obligation, and should do nothing. The CEO, however, was dedicated to the comfort and safety of the children who used the company's furniture, and he insisted on remedies.

He told this to his management team, adding, "We now have two choices. One, we can invent a system that will prevent this from ever happening again, find every piece of this furniture that we have sold in the last ten years, and give every owner an upgrade. Two, we can admit to ourselves and everyone who deals with us that we have been lying about why we are in this business."

Colleen agreed on a logical level that the company was not responsible for the accident. Finding every owner would be an enormous task. A newly ordered computer system was not yet in place, so someone would have to comb through ten years of files and address notices to every owner. A revamped safety system would have to be designed, produced, and shipped. It would involve a lot of work and expense; and they were not responsible for the child's injury.

After much internal turmoil and "soul searching," Colleen finally agreed that no matter the work and expense, no matter whether they were responsible, it had to be done.

She said, "We must do this. We must do it for the safety of the children. We must also do it for our own souls and for the soul of this company."

SPIRIT AND SOUL

In our culture, we use the terms *spirit* and *soul* almost interchangeably, and we lose the richness of our spiritual lives by blurring the distinction. Psychologists James Hillman and Thomas Moore, among others, are attempting to help us recapture that richness. Hillman believes that spirit and soul are reflected respectively in our concepts of "peaks" and "vales." He wrote, "The clamber up the peaks is in search of or is the drive of the spirit in search of the self" (1989, 114). In this sense our view of organizational life as a ladder to climb, or as a place to achieve new heights, provides an opportunity for the spirit to do its labor.

"Soul," said Moore, "is not a thing, but a quality or a dimension of experiencing life and ourselves. It has to do with depth, value, relatedness, heart, and personal substance" (1992, 5).

We have blurred the distinction between spirit and soul partly because spirit is more akin to Newtonianism, rational understanding and transcendence of physical limits. Newtonianism has a way of satisfying the aspirations of spirit but not of soul. Soul defies logic and rationality; it shuns order, so we have lost it, especially in institutions that worship logic, rationality, and order. Soul is too slippery to pin down. Moore stated, "It is impossible to define precisely what the soul is. Definition is an intellectual enterprise anyway; the soul prefers to imagine" (1992, *xi*).

Hillman said, "Spirit is after ultimates." Spirit requires passion. "Soul," on the other hand, "is imagination" (1989, 122). So to the degree that we welcome emotion and imagination into our work, we imbue work with the possibility of both spirit and soul. *All work is spiritual work* means that all work contains the energy of both spirit and soul.

Welcoming spirit and soul into our work is a step in the direction of artfulness. The next steps include developing "centering consciousness" and learning to make the necessary "leaps" from the mundane aspects of our work to their spiritual aspects.

PARTICIPATING AND NONPARTICIPATING CONSCIOUSNESS

Science historian Morris Berman wrote:

> For more than 99 percent of human history, the world was enchanted and man saw himself as an integral part of it. The complete reversal of this perception in a mere four hundred years or so has destroyed the continuity of the human experience and the integrity of the human psyche. It has very nearly wrecked the planet as well. The only hope,

or so it seems to me, lies in a reenchantment of the world. (1984, 10)

I particularly like Berman's characterization of the pre-Newtonian universe as a place of enchantment, a world of spirit and soul. I often think of artists as the keepers of enchantment, struggling to maintain contact with a universe that is alive and soaked in meaning.

Berman described the pre-Newtonian world as the product of "participating consciousness," a way of seeing in which "rocks, trees, rivers, and clouds were all seen as wondrous, alive, and human beings felt at home in this environment" (1984, 2). Participating consciousness views human beings in a reciprocal relationship with the natural world wherein everything exists for some spiritual purpose and carries spiritual meaning.

During the scientific revolution the notion of participating consciousness was shattered and replaced with what Berman called "nonparticipating consciousness." From the perspective of nonparticipating consciousness, our selves are separate from the universe. The foundation of this paradigm is objectivity — we are required to see ourselves as living in a world in which we who are "in here" view objects that are "out there." This is a strict, dualistic way of seeing: rigid distinctions are drawn between observer and observed, between subject and object, between mind and feeling, human and nature.

When we live in a state of nonparticipating consciousness, which dominates our thinking, things do not possess spiritual meaning or purpose; they possess only characteristics and behavior to be measured, manipulated in experiments, and, ultimately, controlled.

In the realm of physics, objectivity died but was not buried in 1927. In that year physicist Werner Heisenberg rediscovered participating consciousness when he articulated his "Uncertainty Principle." Heisenberg's principle holds that the consciousness and behavior of the experimenter are part of the experiment (1971). His great insight was that there is no such thing as an independent observer, thus objectivity is a myth.

In most organizations, the belief in objectivity is, of course, still very much alive. We strive to create objective performance appraisal systems. We believe we can objectively measure customer satisfaction, the impact of a training program, quality, organizational climate, and business trends. We businesspeople assume objectivity; the assumption is so deeply embedded that to question it seems heretical.

CENTERING CONSCIOUSNESS

What of artful work? Can we properly call it either participating or nonparticipating? What does it say about objectivity? What of meaning and purpose? M. C. Richards called the artist's consciousness "centering consciousness" and described how it functions in poetry:

> Centering consciousness in poetry brings together those experiences and objects which appear separate, finding in the single moment of felt-perception a variety of elements simultaneously aglow. As language art, it occupies a realm where through the mysteries of speech, the multiple forms of perception fuse, transcending every single sense, and both space and time. (1989, 67)

The multiple forms of perception Richards described include sense perception and perception of the spiritual.

Centering consciousness is clearly not Newtonian. There is no concern for objectivity. The fact that the artistic view has remained alive alongside the prevailing paradigm is testimony to its resilience and utility. It is also not pre-Newtonian. There is none of the primitive superstition often associated with pre-Newtonian thought. No ghosts, ghouls, goblins, or gremlins.

One limitation of pre-Newtonian consciousness was a lack of awareness that other forms of consciousness existed. A gift of the Newtonian paradigm is that we now know about both participating and nonparticipating consciousness, and knowing that opens the door to other possibilities as well.

Like our pre-Newtonian ancestors, the artist in centering consciousness sees the self as a participant in the universe. However, the artist participates in an alliance with something beyond the physical form; something beyond the rational, beyond the logical; something evocative, emotional, and spiritual. The artist participates in the unseen world, the world that exists beneath or within the physical world, the mysterious world that intersects with the physical world but is not immediately apparent. This world contains invisible forces that shape reality much as the invisible wind shapes trees, rocks, and mountains.

In our organizational activity, we are usually busy maintaining nonparticipating consciousness; splitting work and family apart, men and women apart; severing emotion from intellect, body from soul; separating ourselves into divisions and departments, management and workers; disconnecting work from its deeper meaning; ripping up things into ever smaller pieces to be measured and controlled. Centering consciousness would have us awaken to our experience of the phenomena we try so desperately to keep apart, and find wholeness.

LEAPING

Poet Robert Bly described how centering consciousness functions in what he called "leaping poetry." Leaping poetry at one moment presents something concrete, but then, in the very next moment, leaps to pronounce a mystery of the poet's interior world (1975).

For example, a man named Michael made his reputation in a large consumer products company by rescuing failing pieces of the business. He was, however, not happy in his work and decided to change jobs. He capitalized on his well-deserved reputation and his considerable skill by creating his own consulting business. Within weeks of resigning from the company he had secured several lucrative contracts, acquired a Mercedes, and moved his family to Beverly Hills. He couldn't understand why he still wasn't happy.

One Friday afternoon, returning home from a visit with a client, Michael found himself inching along the San Diego Freeway. He regarded his new car, trapped like a sleek animal in a herd of animals so thick and constrained it was able to move forward only very slowly. He looked at the forlorn grayish yellow air hanging above him like a translucent shroud. Then he looked at himself in the rear-view mirror.

The words passed through him, not a thought exactly. It was more like a memory or one of those images that comes to us when we are waking or falling asleep: This is a place where souls go to die. The "place" was the San Diego Freeway and, at the same time, his own unhappiness with his work.

What Michael experienced was the leap about which Bly spoke: the immediate visceral connection between the mundane and the spiritual. Michael canceled the remainder of his contracts, sold the Mercedes, moved his family to a soul-nurturing environment and found soul-nurturing work. He and his family returned to their New England roots, where he now directs a university business school.

65

Bly stated that "leaping is the ability to associate fast" (1975, 4). The associations occur among objects or experiences in the physical world and the interior world of mystery and meaning. Leaping occurs between the physical and the spiritual. This leaping ability is fundamental to the consciousness of artists. It is about everyday things, such as typing a letter, paying the bills, writing a shopping list, sitting in a traffic jam, or applying paint to canvas. At the same time it is about emotion and spirit. This form of consciousness is about *why* we do what we do. Newtonian, nonparticipating consciousness is about *how* we do what we do; it is about technique but not about spirit.

The artist knows that the world of physical forms contains meaning, meaning that requires a leap. Tending a garden is about nurturing the soul. The artist knows there is a structure to the world which does not appear on its surface. It is a structure of meaning.

The artist may believe the decline of a petroleum company is about healing the earth. Downsizing suggests a return to self-reliance. A performance appraisal is about believing that others hold the secret to your own self-worth. Developing a new product is about seeking joy. Creating a long-range plan implies believing the universe is predictable.

Like Colleen, the artist knows that an accident involving a physically handicapped child, injured by falling from a piece of furniture intended to keep the child comfortable and safe, is not simply about logically deciding who is responsible; it is about her own soul and the soul of her company.

And, like Michael, the artist knows that work that provides no joy, and work environments that stifle spirit, are places where souls go to die.

Do you sense the leaps?

Do you make those leaps when you think about your work?

Does the company you work for encourage such leaps?

THE TALE OF THE TEDDY BEAR

The renaissance in today's business universe offers an opportunity to resurrect soul and thus imbue our work with deeper meaning and commitment.

Here is a story about George, who nurtured soul in the workplace. He managed the marketing division of a heavy equipment company. George was much admired and loved by the people who worked for him; but his division was eliminated and his colleagues were scattered during a reorganization. He asked me to help him design their last meeting, a two-day event.

"What do you want to accomplish at this meeting?" I asked.

George replied, "There is a lot of anger and sadness about this. My people feel frustrated, cheated, and scared. I'd like to do something that helps them get past all that and get on with their lives in other parts of the company."

"Sounds like you want a funeral," I said, surprising even myself.

He laughed. "Yes, I do. But I also want a celebration of what we have done together and the great time we've had doing it."

He was asking for an observance of the soul. Thomas Moore wrote:

Care of the soul begins with observance of how the soul manifests itself
and how it operates. We can't care for the soul unless we are familiar
with its ways. Observance is a word from ritual and religion. It means
to watch out for but also to keep and honor, as in the observance of a
holiday. (1992, 5)

The first morning of the meeting was, indeed, a funeral — a celebratory, New Orleans-style funeral, replete with minister, funeral director, organ-
ist, wreaths, and sermon. They sang the Rolling Stones song, "You Can't
Always Get What You Want." There was a small, plain wooden casket. The
group had a mascot, a Gund teddy bear that they used at important meetings and passed from person to person. The teddy bear was in the casket. A
New Orleans jazz band led them in a procession from the meeting room to a
shallow grave in the woods. Forty people, men and women, salespeople and
engineers, bright-eyed novices, and crusty old dudes, stood at the grave
laughing, crying, hugging one another, remembering, and saying good-bye to
what they had been. They buried the bear. For the rest of the meeting they
talked about the future.

In a wooded place in central New York State, a Gund teddy bear lies in
a grave, silently attesting to the power of soul.

This story teaches us that soulfulness requires the ability to experience
whatever is happening, especially strong emotions. Hillman and Moore are
both clear in their writing that disturbing emotions, in particular, are symptoms that the soul is in trouble. Acknowledging, expressing, and valuing these

67

emotions not only summons the power of emotion to the workplace but also increases the potential for artful and soulful work.

GENIUS AND THE DIVINE

The spirituality of an artist revolves around the relationship between the artist's sense of the divine and the artist's own genius. The call to artful work is thus a call to cultivate our own sense of the divine, become intimate with our own genius, and explore the relationship between the two.

The artist does not normally take full responsibility for inspired work but honors it as a gift from the divine. Contemporary theologian Matthew Fox wrote, "We are thoroughly part of a Greater Work. . . ." (1994, 128). It is this sense that the artist holds, this sense of participating with the divine in the dance that creates creation. It is up to each of us to determine or experience this for ourselves.

The artist also is charged with the responsibility of honoring his or her own personal genius. I use the term *genius* not in the modern sense of brilliant intellect, talent, or characteristic of personality. I use it in the more traditional sense of spirit attending each person and forming each person's gift. Genius is a gift in two ways: it is a gift from the divine to each person and a gift from each person to creation. M. C. Richards, as mentioned earlier, views herself as a "sower of seeds" and describes her seeds — ideas, poems, pottery, books, expressions of her inner self — as her gifts.

Coomaraswamy wrote, "No man . . . can be a genius: but all men have a genius, to be served or disobeyed at their own peril" (1956, 38).

I believe that my own genius lies in "creating clarity," which means examining things that are familiar but not well understood. So I develop theoretical models, consult, teach, write, and seek the perfect photograph. These endeavors are talents through which my genius manifests itself.

The centering consciousness of artful work will allow us to escort spirit and soul, emotion and imagination, into our organizations, and to make the leaps between the intangible and the more mundane aspects of our work. It will encourage us to experience the deeper meaning of our endeavors and recognize our own unique gifts. This is a path toward true long-term commitment to organizational purpose, to deeply held values, and to such lofty and mysterious aspirations as service and quality.

OWNING THE WORK PROCESS

7

To yield means both to lose and to gain.

The fifth belief of artful work is: *artful work demands that the artist owns the work process.* Art and work became separated when workers lost ownership of their own work processes to mechanization and to its human equivalents, hierarchy and bureaucracy.

ART IS DOING

Art is "doing"; it is as much process as product. The joy of artful work arises from the doing. The artist's product, as elegant, as marketable, as profitable as it may be, is the fruit of a process the artist creates. When the process arises from the demands of a factory floor, or the dictates of a manager, hierarchy, or bureaucracy, the possibility for artfulness dies a quiet, devastating death.

Coomaraswamy said it this way:

The mechanical product may still be a work of art: but the art was not the workman's, nor the workman an artist, but a hireling; and this is one of the many ways an "industry without art is brutality." (1956, 35)

Artists decide which tools they require, purchase them, oversee their use, and choose what kind of training they need and how to get it. No one else manages their time. Artists do not do this to express a yearning for freedom, but out of the knowledge that artful work resides in process, and that working artfully requires ownership of the work process.

Artists adhere to restraints, prescriptions, and contracts, just like the rest of us. Photographers know about the limits imposed by light and film. Potters know what they can and cannot do with a lump of clay. Writers know how long a book you are likely to read. Every canvas has edges. Every practicing artist has customers to satisfy.

Owning the work process is not about freedom from restraint but about discovering joy in a process invented as much for the pursuit of joy as for the creation of a product.

We have made strides toward stimulating artful work by ceding ownership of work processes to workers themselves. Our efforts, which are usually referred to as "empowerment," often meet with two resistances. These resistances are based on illusions — the illusion of control and the illusion that an organization is capable of taking care of us.

SURRENDER AND THE ILLUSION OF CONTROL

We maintain an illusion of control when we put Sally's name in a certain box on the organizational chart: Sally sits at the correct desk, uses the correct phone, copy machine, and coffee station; she dresses in the right clothes, attends the right meetings, turns in the right reports, and talks to the right people. I say this is an illusion of control because, although Sally does all of those things, she remains in charge of what she thinks, how she feels, and whether she truly engages her spirit and soul with her work. At best Sally does bring all of her energy to her work. At worst she relinquishes hope for enriching work, succumbs to the "carrot" of extrinsic rewards, gives up expecting to bring her entire self to her work, and stops expecting her work to be joyful.

I met a man whose company gains much recognition and praise because it shares all its financial information with every employee. Every employee has received training about how to read a balance sheet. Employee teams make financial decisions usually reserved only for those at the top of the hierarchy. Proudly, this man told me of one employee team that had the opportunity to pay itself bonuses. The team chose instead to invest in new equipment that would increase quality and productivity.

The company was on the verge of closing its doors just before management decided to involve everybody in the financial operation of the company. It is now a major success story.

When asked what prompted the management of the company to share all of their information and give up so much control, he said, "We surrendered."

"Surrender." It is an interesting word to ponder. It connotes ending a struggle one cannot possibly win; in this case, the struggle to maintain the illusion of control. It seems the managers of the company admitted their defeat in the battle to control the minds, hearts, and spirits of their people. The people, given the opportunity, took charge of their work processes and made a success of the enterprise.

74

This story illustrates the difficulty many managers have with the notion that workers ought to be in charge of their own work processes. To managers, it feels like giving up, or giving in, losing control. Note that the managers didn't surrender until they felt desperate.

Surrender does not appear to be a simple act for those of us raised in Western traditions. Our egos won't allow it. To the extent that we inhabit Newtonianism we are vulnerable to the demands of our relentlessly controlling egos, which emerge from our self-declared position as dominators of the natural world. We are often in a battle to make the world and other people conform to our own wills.

Surrender means you lost, doesn't it? My dictionary (*Random House College Dictionary*, 1975) states that surrender means "to yield to the possession or power of another." There is the magic word — power. Those who currently hold power will have to surrender, no matter how frightening or unnatural it seems, if they want the benefits of artful work — empowerment, engagement, and commitment to visions and values.

What exactly is being surrendered? It is the illusion that we control the energy of others. In other words, what is being surrendered is virtually nothing. If we choose to throw open the doors of our organizations to the fullness of mental, emotional, and spiritual energy, we surrender only the illusion that we ever controlled them.

MEASUREMENT AND CONTROL

Our historical reliance on objective measurement has been an attempt to hold on to the illusion of control. We tend to believe that if we can measure something we can control it. If we persist in compulsive measurement, we ought to at least be careful about how we measure, what we measure, and what we do with our measurements. We ought to acknowledge that our measures are only our measures, not truth, and acknowledge that we cannot adequately measure emotion and spirit, but they are present in our workplaces nonetheless.

A pharmaceutical salesman tells the following story about measurement gone awry. His company, in an attempt to improve the effectiveness of its sales force, decided to count how many doctors each salesman saw each month. This luckless man, who was one of the company's most successful salesmen, was called on the carpet by his boss because the number of doctors he visited was lower than that of other, less successful salesmen.

His boss said, "You are a terrific salesman. Just think how much more you could sell if you saw more doctors."

The salesman had a difficult time convincing his boss that the reason he sold so much was that he took more time to educate the doctors about his products and to understand their needs; thus he saw fewer doctors and sold more pharmaceuticals. His success was not based on how many doctors he saw but on the quality of his relationships with the doctors he did see and on the degree of trust they had in him. This is, of course, much more difficult to measure. It is impossible to be objective about trust.

When what we are doing is not working, and we believe in what we are doing, we try doing it harder. It is a human tendency. During my first visit to Europe, in Frankfurt, Germany, I asked an old man in a checkered shirt and flat cap for directions. He did not speak English. I spoke louder — in English. I *believed* in English, but it didn't work. That is what we do with measurement. When it doesn't provide what we need, we usually decide to measure harder. We measure harder instead of conceding that measurement will help us solve only the more mundane problems.

When the ground beneath our feet begins to slide, we naturally grab hold of whatever is nearest. Sometimes, however, whatever is nearest will not support us; we must reach further. Our current challenges are not challenges of measurement but challenges of emotion and spirit. Measurement alone will not support us; we must reach further.

We also tend to believe our measures are truth. They aren't — they are merely a quantification of what we see. A painter uses the brush handle and thumb to estimate the distance between a model's knee and ankle, knowing what is being measured is not truth but perception. In organizational circles, however, we often treat our measurements as truth, as if they are solid and real, and we treat emotion and spirit as if they are soft and unreal. Currently, hard wins over soft.

What we measure is not truth; it is merely what we measure. In the physical realm, good measurement ensures that the expensive piece of oak I subject to my saw will fit the space I want it to fit. In the human realm, measurement ensures only that we have new information or confirmation about what we have already decided is important.

Poets measure syllables. Painters measure distances. Carpenters measure wood and space. Writers measure sentences, paragraphs, and pages.

Managers measure performance. Investors measure profits. Doctors measure pathology and health.

We measure only what we value and are in danger when what we value is measurement itself.

Measurement is a consequential facet of work processes and of artfulness. Measurement is a tool, a technique. It needs to be firmly in the grip of the worker who aspires to artfulness.

77

Our choice is control or surrender. We can see now that control is largely an illusion. Surrender means relinquishing this illusion. It means giving in to artful work, owning our own work processes, and understanding that measurement alone is inadequate to meet our challenges.

THE ILLUSION THAT WE WILL BE "TAKEN CARE OF"

Another illusion that spawns our resistance to owning our work processes is the illusion that a company will take care of us.

A chemical engineering company offers a career development training program to its employees. The company created the program because it was reorganizing and downsizing, resulting in fewer opportunities for upward mobility. In this company, historically, those at the top of the hierarchy managed each employee's career. People went to work there, did their jobs, and senior managers held endless rounds of long and secretive meetings to decide their workers' fates.

Reorganization and downsizing played havoc with tradition. There were fewer career options. Managers, inheriting wider spans of control and more subordinates, couldn't keep up with the careers of people they managed. Employees, used to having their careers looked after, hadn't a clue about how to manage their own careers and were resentful that the managers weren't doing it for them anymore.

The aim of the training program was to help employees understand the situation, take responsibility for their own careers, and learn the attitudes and skills required for successful career management. During the early stages of the training program, participants often vented anger and frustration about the message that their career was essentially in their hands.

Because we have traditionally placed in the hands of managers power over careers, and employees have had the dubious luxury of not having to contend with such things, employees often feel resentful and angry when they actually have to contend with assuming control.

The same is true for work processes. Power over work processes has historically been placed in the hands of managers. Again, employees feel resentful and angry when they have to deal with work processes themselves. During one training program a young engineer said, "I came to this company to do engineering, not to manage my career or my work. I thought that once I decided to come here, all that other stuff would be taken care of."

In chapter 3 I wrote about actors going off book. At some point during rehearsals, the director will say something like, "I want everybody off book by next Wednesday." It means that the actors will rehearse then without the script in their hands. Remember, an actor who goes off book must do three things: be authentic while performing the role in the play, inhabit the structure of the play, and create the play.

Anyone who works for an organization and who aspires to artfulness must do the same: be authentic while performing the role that the organization requires, inhabit the structure of the organization, and create the organization.

In today's organizational environment, there is little prospect that anyone will be "taken care of." Believing that is another illusion that yields resistance to owning one's work processes and to artful work. We will each have to manage our own work and cherish the responsibility of creating the organization where we work.

Cherishing responsibility for creating organizations that support artful work means assuming our share of responsibility for the purpose and culture of that organization. So many of us relinquish that responsibility to those we see as leaders, denying that whatever we do contributes to the degree of artfulness around us.

In a training program designed to help people empower themselves, a participant said, "I get it! When I complain about management and act powerless, I contribute to a culture of powerlessness. Even when I remain silent, I contribute to how this company feels. The only way to create the kind of organization I want to be part of is to behave as if it already exists."

I WANT EVERYBODY OFF BOOK BY NEXT WEDNESDAY!

A NEW COVENANT

The historical covenant between companies and employees has vanished. The covenant held that companies would agree to provide security and external rewards, while employees agreed to engage in work for which they had little or no intrinsic motivation and where they experienced little or no joy.

Artful work suggests an alternative. It is a new covenant in which companies pledge to provide joyful work and surrender control of work processes. This pledge encourages artful work and increases the possibility that employees will commit to quality, values, and service. This covenant requires that companies be very clear about their purposes and create new processes to link people with joyful work. Employees agree to take charge of their own careers, depend for security on their own skills and resources, and resolutely seek artful work and ownership of their work processes.

80

USE OF THE SELF

8

We are poems in the making.

The sixth and seventh beliefs of artful work are, like the second and third, closely related. They are about how we use ourselves while at work and about how the work affects us. They are: *artful work requires consistent and conscious use of the self,* and *as the artist creates the work, the work creates the artist.*

THE WALL

Sixteen people stand on frozen earth in a semicircle at the top of a wooded slope. It is February, it is Canada, and the air is cold enough to create dense puffs of white breath. They are dressed in ski jackets, bulky sweaters, scarves, mittens, and boots. Although it is cold, they are stock still, listening. Listening as if their lives depended on listening. Such intense concentration is a new experience for some of them.

Before them is a twelve-foot-high, smooth-faced wall of plywood. At the top of the wall a man perches on a narrow platform mounted a few feet below the top on the opposite side from where they stand. He is visible to them only from the waist up. It is this man they listen to.

"The object of this exercise is to get the entire group up and over the wall." They appraise the wall with unbelieving eyes. They do not look at one another. They do not make a sound.

They are a diverse group but have this in common: they work for the same company, and that company has invited them to engage in this experience as a way to forge a common sense of purpose among its people. This wall is the last challenge in three days of such challenges.

The man at the top of the wall explains the rules: no props may be used and everyone is responsible for ensuring the safety of those who have their feet off the ground. If anyone breaks the safety rule, the entire group must begin again.

This last rule elicits groans from the group. They have had experience over the prior few days with making mistakes and starting over. They do not like starting over and are not used to having their performance scrutinized, or to being held to such exacting "no-mistakes" standards.

Finally the man tells them, "You will have ninety minutes to complete this challenge. I suggest you develop a plan."

For a moment they do not move; they stare at the wall. Then they emit a collective sigh of resignation and slowly begin to move, closing the semicircle, standing now in a complete circle. The wall, the man, and the cold are now outside their attention as they focus on one another and on the challenge they face.

Similar scenes have recently become commonplace in organizational training. They provide what is called *experiential learning*. After the group attempted the challenge, they walked to the nearest warm place and discussed, or "debriefed," their experience. During the debriefing they learned about teamwork, leadership, planning, communication, vision, and commitment; mostly, however, they learned about themselves.

TASK, PROCESS, AND THE INTERIOR LIFE

I have facilitated many debriefings of experiential learning activities and have often been delighted and astounded by the depth of learning that emerges. People experience deep feelings and talk together about challenges to the spirit. Deep feelings arise when we attend to our interior lives.

Conventional wisdom about these groups holds that group members should address two things during a debriefing: the task itself and the process used to attempt the task. The questions raised in debriefings are usually variations on these two — What did we do? and How did we do it? Task and process. Those of us who attend debriefings as coaches know that the typical team will underestimate the value of considering their process. Unless urged, they usually will not talk about how they made decisions, how effective or dysfunctional their communication was, or whether the group gave adequate attention to ideas.

Because we now recognize that quality requires favorable processes, we are beginning to give more consideration to process. Still, our attention tends to focus more on manufacturing or work processes rather than on the subtle and delicate processes that occur among human beings. In hierarchical organizations, we have usually settled questions of human processes by carefully observing how the boss responds.

84

Artists know that there is yet a third element penetrating their work: the interior world of the worker, the world of emotion and spirit. The following quotation from M. C. Richards expresses this aspect of artistry:

> Where should I attach the handle to this pitcher? The question here lies in the "should." What does it mean, "should"? What kind of handle do I want? I don't know. I don't know. What does it mean, "I don't know"? It means there are many different kinds of considerations, and I don't know how to satisfy them all. I want the handle to be strong enough to support the weight of the pitcher when it is filled. I want to be able to get my hand through it. I want it to be placed so that it does not weaken the wall and crack the pot, and so that the balance of the pitcher is good in the pouring. I want it to make a beautiful total shape. I want it to be my handle at the same time that I want to please my customer, my friends, my critics, whomever. And in another impulse I don't care about any of these things: I want it to be a complete surprise. Poetry often enters through the window of irrelevance. So if the handle does not satisfy any of the above requirements, the pot may have a certain marvelous charm, an original image: a cracked pitcher that carries in it the magic of the

self-forgetful impulse which in a rage of joy and irreverence stuck the handle on in something of the spirit in which we pin the tail on the donkey blindfolded. A glee, an energy, that escapes from all those questions-and-answers, thumbs its nose, stands on the ridgepole, and crows like a cock for its own dawning. What is this all about? These different moods sweep through us. How much authority should we give them? To be solemn to be merry to be chaste to be voluptuous to be reserved to be prodigal to be elegant to be vulgar to be tasteful to be tasteless to be useful to be useless to be something to be nothing to be alive in this weather. (1989, 10–11)

This is Richards debriefing herself. She is debriefing her task, process, and interior life in an integrated way — all at once. The company employees debriefing their experience about the wall are usually surprised and chagrined by how much interior life they ignored while engaged in their task, and by how much the interior life affected their success or failure.

They are surprised and chagrined, for example, to discover that a woman who had done the task before never revealed that fact because, within herself, she decided she might ruin the group's experience. She was ambivalent about what to do. She did not express her ambivalence and leave the choice to the group; she made it herself.

They are surprised and chagrined to discover that a man was angry at another man who assumed leadership. The angry man withdrew; he offered no ideas and only halfheartedly participated. Other people wondered why he seemed so uninvolved, so detached. No one asked.

This is the interior life at work. The emotional and spiritual undercurrent.

It is always present. It is rarely, in work settings, used to anyone's advantage. Consistent and conscious use of the self suggests that we express the undercurrent and convert it into constructive energy.

CONSISTENT AND CONSCIOUS USE OF THE SELF

Consistent and conscious use of the self in work requires that we become intimate with our own interior world. This is, of course, a lifelong task. Consistent and conscious use of the self does not mean dragging skeletons out of the family closet or turning our workplaces into quasi-therapeutic communities. It means becoming more practiced at sensing our emotions, imagination, spirit, and soul, our dreams, reflections, and reveries while at work, and using the energy they contain to move our work forward.

Intimacy with our own interior world means that we are aware of it and recognize its validity. It means that we embrace and value the contents of our inner life as signals of our contact with the world around us.

For example, when we feel frustration while solving a problem, it often means that we are close to a solution. Frustration might also signal that we ought to try something new. Acknowledging the emotion of frustration can be useful.

Fear often means that we are facing a real threat. Acknowledging the emotion of fear can be useful, too.

Joy means that we are in the presence of something good for us. Acknowledging joy can be useful. Excitement is part challenge and part fear. We will not feel excited about our work without acknowledging fear. Commitment is the deep feeling that we must do what we must do. We cannot be committed without feeling. Values are those abstract qualities that we care about. We cannot commit to values without caring.

The examples above demonstrate conscious use of the energy of emotion. Here is a story about conscious use of the energy of spirit.

I once attended the first meeting of a project team. The team leader, Dan, asked each of us to speak briefly about why we wanted to be part of that team. He asked us what we were hoping to achieve. He explained that he believed the team had a better chance of success if we all knew what we hoped to accomplish together, as well as what we each hoped to accomplish for ourselves as a member of the team.

Dan was acknowledging spirit. A woman spoke of her desire to make a difference for a company she truly loved. A man spoke of a deeply felt need to expand his knowledge. Another man said he believed the project had important consequences beyond the company, that the team's work had the potential to improve life for many people.

SAFETY FOR THE WHOLE PERSON

Besides bringing our interior lives to work, consistent and conscious use of the self also requires encouraging those around us to give voice to their interior lives. This does not involve playing amateur psychologist. The point of encouraging others to give voice to their interior lives is not to fix people or solve personal problems. The point is to bring the powerful energy of the interior life to the task at hand.

We work hard to create physical safety in our workplaces. Can we also create mental, emotional, and spiritual safety — safety for the whole person?

WORKING WITH WHAT IS

Consistent conscious use of the self within work also requires learning to utilize the energy of the interior world to move our work forward.

My interior voice wonders about you. Who are you? What do you want from me? I want this to be my book, and I want it to interest and stimulate you. At the moment I have only my own interior sense of you to rely on for answers to my questions. I acknowledge my fear that you will think this book is either "too far out" or not far enough. I acknowledge my frustration that I cannot see and respond to your reactions as you read my words. I do not wish to be misunderstood. I acknowledge my fondness for living on the boundary of whatever wave is cresting and that this fondness often creates feelings of alienation and aloneness.

My fears, frustrations, and fondness for boundaries grip my writing. If I struggle against the grip, or if I deny it, this writing will become a battle for me and will produce arid, lifeless writing for you. If I acknowledge the grip, slide into it, use it as a martial artist uses the energy of his or her opponent, I have a better chance of producing artful work.

In your work, what is it that you need to slide into? Fear? Frustration? The knowledge that your work demands more compromise than your soul can make? A stifling of your spirit? The sense that you are the only one in your organization who sees the truth? Is there something you see that everyone around you seems to deny? Do you believe that your company's products are destructive? Do you sense that everyone around you feels frightened, lonely, detached? Slide into those feelings. Slide into them and use the energy of the slide to create movement in your workplace.

Thomas Moore, writing about observing the soul, stated, "You take back what has been disowned. You work with what is, rather than what you wish were there" (1992, 9).

Consistent and conscious use of the self means taking back our disowned feelings and spiritual longings. It means treating unpleasant emotions as clues that some kind of healing is occurring or is required. It means observing the manifestations of spirit and soul. It means listening and seeing what is being revealed to us by our interior lives. Finally, it means using the meaning we gain through observing these mysteries to create work and organizations where artfulness will thrive.

All of this can be done only by working with what *is* rather than what we *wish were there*.

HERDING A BEAR

A poet drives a battered blue truck along a narrow, rutted, wooded road. He is seeking the solitude of a bright stream and a small clearing in the trees. In front of him and to his right lopes a large brown bear. The bear veers left to cross the road, spies the truck, changes course again, and disappears into a thick stand of mountain laurel. The poet slows the truck, brings it alongside the laurel, and peers into the dense foliage. The bear waits no more than twenty feet away. The poet wonders if he has frightened the bear. They study each other for a long, tense moment.

The bear begins running again, keeping to its original course. It seems to want to cross the road and knows it will have to outrun the truck to do so. The poet eases the truck into gear and follows, wheels caught by the ruts in the road, keeping the bear to his right. Again the bear stops, in the open this time. The bear senses no threat and merely wants to cross the road. The poet intends no threat and is awed and amused by the bear. He is herding the bear in order to savor the sight of an impressive, magical creature.

Once again the poet and bear regard each other. To the poet, the bear looks tired and annoyed.

Then, reluctantly, the poet shifts the truck into reverse and backs slowly away, leaving a clear path for the bear to cross. He backs up the truck about thirty feet and waits.

A few moments pass. The old but well-tuned truck idles softly. Then the bear emerges onto the road. It stops, turns its sizable head toward the poet sitting in the truck. The poet expects the bear to enter the woods on the opposite side of the road. But, after examining the truck, seeking perhaps the poet's motive and intention, the bear turns and saunters away down the center of the road. The bear did not want to cross the road; the bear wanted the road to itself. The poet watches the bear leave, then waits a full ten minutes, allowing the bear a measure of solitude. The poet and the battered blue truck then continue down the road.

Later, the poet writes about his encounter with the bear. Why did he herd the bear? He senses his own insensitivity. He sees that his curiosity caused him, perhaps, to frighten the bear. Does he have any right to frighten a bear, for any reason? Why did he stop following the bear? Why back away? Kindness? *Am I kind?* the poet asks himself. *Am I kind to those around me, never mind bears in the woods? What is the meaning of a bear in the woods? For that matter, what is the meaning of a poet in the woods? Did I have any*

90

damn business herding the bear? Did I frighten it?

As the poet does his work, he changes. As he makes use of his interior life of feelings, curiosity, and concern for bears, questions and answers, he comes to a new understanding of himself, of insensitivity and kindness, and of bears. He decides not to herd bears in the woods again and to be more kind to those around him.

When we bring our interior life to our work, whatever the work, the work changes us. It changes us profoundly, in all aspects of our lives, as it changed the poet. It changes us as workers and as human beings.

THE WORK CREATES THE ARTIST

A manager has a report to write for a group of executives. This is not as dramatic as stumbling across a bear in the woods, but it is his work. He wonders, *What do they want to hear?* He suspects they do not want to hear what he wants to say. He suspects they want to be herded in the direction they are already going. He believes he blocks their path at his own peril. *What do they want to hear? What do I want to say? How can I say what I want to say in a way that does not sound self-promoting? What is the risk of being who I am?* He does not wish to say that he thinks the direction they are headed is foolish. Will he summon the courage of his convictions? He does not wish to commit career suicide by telling the truth of his perception and judgment. If he made use of his interior life, he would say all of this. He has a choice. He might write, "I don't want to tell you this because I am afraid you don't want to hear it and it'll cost me my job." He might also write, "Despite opinion to the contrary . . ."

He wants to use himself, and he wonders who he is supposed to be. He is expected to put aside his interior life, to be other than who he actually is. When he does this, he has little chance to examine how his work is doing him. And he dies a little.

We see work as something we do, not something that does us. This cannot be good for us, and it cannot be good for the organizations that employ us.

It cannot be good for us because all too often we ignore our work's impact on us until the heart attack; the ulcer; the stress-induced break-down; the fracture of the family; the midlife crisis; the cold, hard slap across the face; the latest addiction; or the shock that arouses us from our slumber. We continue to ignore such things as our own insensitivity or lack of kindness. We have a job to do after all! No room for these sentimental musings! No room for an interior life, and if it should somehow surface, it has nothing to do with work!

Our interior life is there, however, often hiding behind the cover of our inner laurel bushes, like a frightened bear.

CREATING ME

Work is a passage of self-discovery. M. C. Richards wrote, "It is not the pots we are forming, but ourselves" (1989, 13).

This work has created me, the me I am today in contrast to the me I was before I began. When I began this writing I was annoyed with all of us, myself included, for our seeming inability or unwillingness to create lasting change in our organizations and to seek joy in our work. As my writing proceeded, I became more compassionate toward all of us, myself included, as well as more forgiving and understanding. It is a difficult thing we are attempting to do — reinvent ourselves.

I also realized that my own worst enemy is moralism. Moralism means becoming emotionally attached to my own assessments of reality, believing I have the truth that will liberate us or provide us with redemption. I am aware of this tendency in myself every time I write the words "we must". I found an adequate, though not wholly satisfying, solution to moralism in the writing of psychotherapist Brad Blanton, who said moralism is "a disease from which we all suffer. It is incurable. It can only be managed and lived with like herpes or diabetes" (1994, 21).

Thanks a lot, Brad! Well, I've done my best to manage my moralism in this writing and I know it still peeks through. I forgive myself for that. I hope you will too.

We believe we are forming the next report to the shareholder, the next performance appraisal, the next product to roll out the door. In reality we are forming ourselves, and the selves we are forming are creating our organizations. It is an endless cycle.

M. C. Richards also wrote, "An act of the self, that's what one must make. An act of the self, from me to you. From center to center. We must mean what we say, from our innermost heart to the outermost galaxy" (1989, 18).

Artful work requires lively involvement. We *can* be ourselves at work. We *can* learn to harness our energies with confidence so that, as we allow ourselves to be more fully human and understand how our work creates us,

93

our efforts together will become more fully what they might be.

When we are willing to acknowledge our whole selves at work, to admit that some work has no meaning to us and offers no possibility of joy, to examine what work will have meaning to us and seek such work, to meet our coworkers self to self, center to center, and to stop pretending that our interior lives don't matter, then our work will become more joyful, and our organizations will flourish with commitment, passion, imagination, spirit, and soul.

94

THE CENTERED ORGANIZATION

9

All the arts we practice are apprenticeship. The big art is our life.

N o organizational work is performed in isolation. An organization consists of people, systems, norms, and a host of other factors that form a context for the work. How we work alters the context, and the context influences how we work. It is a self-reinforcing system.

Our attempts to be artful at our work will be effortless or fruitless to the degree that our organizational context supports or discourages artfulness. If we want to work artfully, we will each need to assume a measure of responsibility for the context in which our work occurs. When we do not take responsibility for creating our own context, we end up inhabiting someone else's. How might it look — a context that supports artful work?

A NOTE OF APPREHENSION

I am apprehensive about this chapter because I am about to describe a mental model of organizational centering after having said that mental approaches alone will not solve our problems in any substantive manner. Artful work values intellect but suggests that we rely too much on intellect to the exclusion of other valuable forms of human energy.

This model is not a solution to anything. It is only a way of looking at organizations. The last thing we ought to do is replace existing ideas about organizations with yet another idea and go on as we have before, believing we have the solution. If it is a good model, it will help us understand something complex and challenging.

Please engage your whole self as you read. In other words, read in a centered way. Be alert to how you feel as you read, as well as to what you think. Does this model annoy or please you? Be alert to your physical self. Does what you read make you squirm? Does it make you frown? Ask yourself questions of spirit, too. What does this have to do with my work, my company, me?

THREE DOMAINS OF ORGANIZATION

All efforts to develop and maintain organizations belong to one of three domains: organizational purpose, organizational culture, and the individual people who constitute the organization.

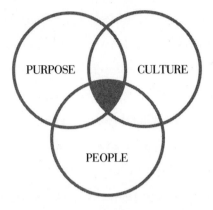

Figure 1: Three Domains of Organizations

Executives, managers, consultants, and others who attempt to improve or maintain organizations, work in the domain of organizational purpose when they talk about the vision, values, or mission of the organization, or puzzle about customers, or about shareholder expectations. Dialogues in this domain are attempts to answer the question, Why does this organization exist?

The domain of organizational culture contains four elements: artifacts, procedures, norms, and climate. Artifacts are anything the organization buys or creates for its own use: for example, furniture, training programs, buildings, or equipment. Procedures are formalized processes, such as policies, strategies, and so forth. Procedures are the written rules of the organization.

Norms are the unwritten rules about what people in the organization are supposed to believe and how they are supposed to behave. Examples are: how decisions are made, how conflict is managed, and how people greet one another.

Climate refers to the current feel of the organization. Is it energetic? Optimistic? Depressed? Why?

Our efforts in the domain of organizational culture are attempts to answer questions such as, How do things work in this organization? What does the organization need? What does it do? How does it feel?

98

These four elements of organizational culture spring from beliefs about how the world works. If the beliefs are consonant with the prevailing Newtonian paradigm, the four elements of culture will reflect that consonance. If the beliefs are more consonant with artful work, the elements of the culture will reflect that consonance instead.

We are in the domain of individual persons, the third circle in the diagram, when we appraise performance, coach, counsel, educate, hire, retire, and so on. Our efforts in this domain are attempts to answer the questions, Who am I? What is expected of me? and How do I contribute to the organization?

As Figure 1 shows, there is some overlap among these three domains, some area where there is alignment and synergy among them. Although our efforts to develop organizations may fall into one or the other of the three domains, the ultimate aim of all such activities is always to increase the size of the area of overlap. For example, the use of personality inventories is not merely for the purpose of enlightening individuals about themselves but also to help people make connections between themselves and the organization's purpose and culture. Such activities increase the harmony between the purpose and culture of the organization and the needs, aspirations, and contributions of individual persons.

ANOTHER DIMENSION OF ORGANIZATION

The information in Figure 1 is not grand news to leaders, managers, or consultants who are well versed in the challenges of creating and maintaining organizations. What may be news, however, is the notion contained in organizational centering: that our efforts will succeed to the degree that we go about them in ways that promote centering. In the words of M. C. Richards, our efforts will succeed if we also succeed at "bringing into center all elements of our sensations and our thinking and our emotions and our will: all the realities of our bodies and our souls" (1989, 36). So there is another dimension to our picture of organizations, shown in Figure 2.

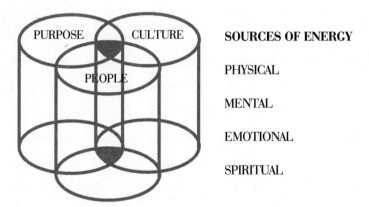

Figure 2: Three Domains and Four Energies in Organizations

This third dimension integrates all four energies: physical, mental, emotional, and spiritual. Figure 2 suggests that we need to proceed with our efforts within the three domains of purpose, culture, and people while incorporating the four levels of human energy. For example, creating a new sense of organizational purpose ought to include attending to what equipment might be needed (physical), how people might need to think differently (mental), how people will feel about the new direction (emotional), and whether the new direction meets the highest aspirations and sense of mission of those who will have to communicate it to others (spiritual).

WELCOMING FEELING AND SPIRIT

Organizational centering is a term that describes all endeavors aimed at bringing the body, mind, emotion, and spirit together in the workplace. Organizational centering involves bringing all the energy of our selves to work and creating organizations where that energy is valued.

The bedrock of organizational centering is that the challenges faced by our organizations will be met to the degree that we succeed at *welcoming* all of our energies beyond the imposing doors that admit us to our workplaces. Until we succeed at organizational centering, all approaches to the challenges that bedevil our organizations are likely to produce only fleeting results.

Often it is as if we drive into the parking lots of our offices or plants, open the trunks of our cars, remove our briefcases, place at least half of our selves in the trunks, then go to work. At the end of the day, we go back to the cars, returning briefcases to trunks. We attempt to reclaim whatever portion of ourselves that withstood being locked away in a dark, airless place, and go home. We have expended physical energy and exercised mental energy, but our emotional energy has been on hold, our spirit suffers, and the challenges remain.

This is very sad. When we delete emotion and spirit from work, we rob ourselves of humanity and deprive our organizations of the energy they require.

Organizational centering is consistent with artful work; they are both invitations to value all forms of human energy. Whenever any of us acts out of centeredness, we contribute to a centered organization. Whenever we do anything that promotes organizational centering we contribute to the possibility for artful work to surface.

CHARACTERISTICS OF A CENTERED ORGANIZATION

A mental image of a centered organization arises from the ideas of artful work and organizational centering. You have discovered by now that this is not a how-to book. The need to work artfully at creating centered organizations will not allow it to be one. If we do not own the work of creating centeredness in our own organizations, we have little hope that our organizations will become centered.

As I have said previously, commitment to purpose is immeasurably more important than technique. When we commit to purpose, we find or invent the elegant technique to meet our purpose. When we focus on technique rather than purpose, our techniques fail us. Or, perhaps, we fail them by using them poorly. The mental image of a centered organization I describe is an attempt to permeate our work and our organizations with new purpose. In other words, I can't describe exactly how to do it, but I can describe how I think it should look. This image also summarizes the relationship between artful work and organizational centering.

The centered organization has the following characteristics:

- **All forms of human energy — physical, mental, emotional, and spiritual — are welcomed, validated, and viewed as a contribution to the organization.**

A sense of safety for the whole person prevails. Emotions and the manifestations of the spirit and soul are present everywhere: on the factory floor, in brochures, in delivery trucks, at every meeting, in every exchange between people, everywhere.

- **Joy is intrinsic to work processes.**

It is expected that work provides joy. The organization as a whole, and each individual, accepts responsibility for discovering joyful work and for matching people with work that contains the possibility of joy.

- **People are involved in work that is congruent with the requirements of their own spirits and souls.**

The organization provides processes that ensure congruence. Employees are conversant about their spiritual needs from work and assume responsibility for seeking work that has spiritual meaning for them.

- **Commitment is the norm.**

Commitment to work is a main criterion for work selection, along with the more traditional criteria of readiness and skill.

- **People manage their own work processes and have the necessary resources to do so.**

Power and information are shared freely. Employees decide what information they want. People manage their own work.

- **Consistent and conscious use of the self pervades all work.**

Unpleasant emotions such as grief and fear are treated as clues that some kind of healing is occurring or is required. Spirit and soul are observed and the meaning gained influences the direction of the organization. When dealing with the interior self, people work with what is rather than what they wish were there. The organization and its work are viewed as vehicles for self-expression and human growth.

- **Decisions are made as much on the basis of feeling, spirit, and soul as on intellect and logic.**

Reverie, dreams, reflections, emotion, intuition, and imagination are discussed freely, as well as the rational "pros and cons." All carry weight in the decision-making process.

- **Technique is always in the service of commitment to purpose.**

Everyone recognizes that technique without commitment to purpose wastes organizational resources. Everyone regularly examines commitment to purpose.

- **Communication flows from one self to another self.**

People talk as much about their personal reactions and feelings toward the task at hand as about the task itself. Honesty is the norm; people say what they mean.

- **People strive to be perceptive, receptive, and expressive.**

Logic is viewed as one tool only. An appreciation for mystery develops. Self-expression is encouraged. Diversity of expression is cherished. Listening is a highly valued skill.

■ **People are engaged with and committed to both the organization's processes and its products.**

Everyone assumes responsibility for creating the context in which artfulness can thrive. People are proud of the organization's products and services.

104

■ **Connections are drawn spontaneously between the mundane aspects of work and the underlying world of meaning.**

There are frequent discussions of the meaning of the organization's work, products, and purpose. People acknowledge that meaning contains issues beyond the immediate concerns or needs of employees, customers, investors, or others. Centering consciousness pervades work. Discussions that leap from the mundane to the spiritual are commonplace.

This image of a centered organization challenges us to explore regions that our present circumstances may tell us do not, or cannot, exist. The image is akin to Henry Moore's secret of life: a task you bring everything to, that you cannot possibly do, and that sustains the questing nature of your spirit.

ARTFUL LEADERSHIP

10

*It takes courage to grow up
and turn out to be who we are.*

Leadership is making dreams come true by activating the energy of others to nourish a collective vision with the necessary concentration and faith. Leadership is both science and art, both technique and magic. Unfortunately those of us who study leadership have tended to focus on the science of leadership and overlooked its artful aspects.

While all work can be artful, leadership absolutely requires artfulness in a way that other work does not, because leadership involves vision and human energy.

"LEADERS DON'T GIVE A DAMN ABOUT ANY OF THIS"

A few colleagues and I created a questionnaire to provide feedback to leaders. We wanted to understand leadership, help others understand it, and develop a product for people who wanted to improve their ability to lead. We created a leadership model and designed a questionnaire and feedback process that has a sound, valid methodology and has proved useful to many people. The questionnaire, like others of its kind, describes behaviors and characteristics of leaders.

During the time we worked on the questionnaire, I felt a vague sense of discomfort about our efforts; something seemed to be missing. I scanned the writings of others who were studying leadership, but that did not calm my disquiet. I couldn't grasp what was wrong. I figured it out at a seminar on writing.

In a crowded, stifling room fifty people are sitting on metal folding chairs at the evening seminar. The leaders are equipped with overhead transparencies showing data they collected during a research study. Somehow they identified the dozen most-admired contemporary American writers and calculated the average number of words per sentence and average number of sentences per paragraph in those writers' works. The presenters believed that writers would maximize their chances of being successful by paying strict attention to these formulas. The bored audience collectively cheered when a woman in the back of the room stood up and said, "Isaac Bashevis Singer is a friend of mine, and I can tell you with absolute certainty that he doesn't give a damn about any of this."

Good writing is not measured solely by the scientific study of average words per sentence. It is acclaimed, but not quantified, for the artistry it contains. While measures like those gathered by the seminar leaders are useful guidelines, merely understanding them is not likely to produce good writing. Certainly if every sentence in this book were longer than, say, twenty words, it is unlikely you would have read this far. However, it is foolish to assume that we can understand writing by measuring it. There is mystery — perhaps magic — within writing and other art forms.

Having tried to be a good scientist about leadership, I seem to hear a voice from the back of the room saying, "*Leaders* don't give a damn about any of this."

Just as good writing is not measured solely by average words per sentence, good leadership is not measured only by how often a person behaves a certain way or by personal characteristics. Leadership cannot be adequately described through Newton's lens. Leadership, like writing, is an art form. When we attend to behaviors and characteristics, we are attending to the surface of leadership.

MAKING DREAMS COME TRUE

Leaders make their dreams, and the dreams of others, come true. A leader's dream is most often called a vision.

Leaders swim in their own emotional and spiritual undercurrents. Visions emanate from the undercurrents. Any particular leader's vision arises within the context of everything that the leader knows about the present and past and from all that can be intuited about the future. Although vision arises within that context, its source is the spiritual energy that works through the leader in the same way it works through a potter at the wheel.

Creating a vision is not a purely rational exercise. Creating a vision is an act of both inspiration and aspiration. As inspiration, the act is "in spirit." The inspiration of the visionary proceeds from a mysterious source and is informed, but not guided, by perceptions of reality. As aspiration, the act of creating a vision expresses a desire to move "toward spirit." The aspiration of the visionary is the dream. It supersedes perceptions of reality. In aspiration, the visionary seeks to create a superior reality to what currently exists.

Creating a vision is an artist's act of deciding both what is to be made and why it is to be made, whether the thing is a product, process, company, or manufacturing plant.

M. C. Richards wrote, "Craftsmen live within a special immediacy in the double realms of these concerns: the questions of technique and the questions of meaning" (1989, 10).

A leader *crafts* a vision, attending to meaning, with consciousness leaping from the physical world to the world of spirit and soul. In the business community, for example, a leader's thinking must go beyond the customer, the stockholder, and the people who work in the business. In what now often passes for organizational visioning, this viewpoint borders on heresy. In what now often passes for organizational visioning, the leader is supposed to be attending to those concerns as well as to quality, safety, cost control, and customer service.

A man who had recently become CEO of a company that leased at-home medical equipment, such as respirators, considered the meaning of both his work and his company's service. Until that time people in the company viewed themselves as technicians who serviced equipment, delivery people who filled orders, managers who oversaw the business, and so forth. In other words, each person's perspective was limited to his or her own work.

The CEO, however, began to see the deeper significance of the company: supporting life. He spoke with many people inside and outside the company and searched himself to discover why he was attracted to his job in the first place. His newly acquired sense of the company's meaning in turn gave meaning to everyone's work.

The needs of customers, stockholders, and employees, as well as the technology of quality, cost control, and service are the surface realities that a leader must visit in order to ensure his or her business's life and health. Those concerns are analogous to the painter's concerns about purchasing quality brushes and paints, matting and framing the work well, pricing it fairly, displaying it attractively in a gallery, and being accessible to buyers. The question that lies beneath the surface is, Why, in the spiritual sense, ought this business (or this painting) live at all?

I have seen many visions printed nicely on fine paper, or etched into acrylic, or framed and hung on a lobby wall. I usually scrutinize them and have a personal test for their worthiness. I know this is arrogant. I do it anyway. The process reminds me of a moment when I was touring the Sistine Chapel and I felt compelled to reach out and touch a patch of beautifully flocked wallpaper. In this way, I feel the texture of a vision.

I scrutinize visions for these commitments: commitment to developing the potency of people, commitment to manifestation of spirit in the work community, and commitment to stewardship of life itself. I have never actually seen those words used in a vision but I can sense their presence or absence.

110

Leaders must also trust their interior voices, especially the small, quiet voice that visits in moments of silence and solitude. This voice does not speak logically, even though it may use words. The voice does not argue, is not critical, and sounds as if it is coming from deep inside or from someplace yet deeper. It may also speak in images and dreams. Robert Henri wrote:

> There are moments in our lives, there are moments in a day, when we
> seem to see beyond the usual — become clairvoyant. We reach then
> into reality. Such are the moments of our greatest happiness. Such are
> the moments of our greatest wisdom. It is in the nature of all people to
> have these experiences; but in our time and under the conditions of
> our lives, it is only a rare few who are able to continue in the experi-
> ence and find expression for it. (1984, 44)

A true visionary strives to become one of those rare few.

CONCENTRATION AND FAITH

Exactly how a leader makes dreams come true is a mystery. The process is akin to art. Somehow, having conceived a vision and, using practiced techniques, a dream comes alive. A painting, a pot, a film, or a poem is born, a war is won, a company transcends its expectations, a person becomes all that he or she can be. A dream transmutes to a concrete reality.

What are we to do with this mystery? We do what we do with all mysteries. We recognize that it is a mystery and not a problem. Because it is not a problem, we do not seek solutions. Rather, we explore it, turn it over and over, examine it.

My own exploration into the mystery of making dreams come true has led me to believe that the process requires at least two elements besides the capacity to create a vision and technical expertise. The process also requires concentration and faith.

M. C. Richards describes her excursion through the secrets of mastering the potter's wheel in this way:

> It took me seven years before I could, with certainty, center any given piece of clay. . . . My task was to learn how to bring in the flying images, how to keep from falling in love with a mistake, how to bring the images in, down, up, smoothly centered, and then to allow them the kind of breath they cannot have if all they know how to be is passionate or repressed. (1989, 11–12)

Seven years of concentration!

Concentration is not merely an exploit of the mind. Concentration is calling our entire self to whatever task we choose — concentration is centering. Leaders are experts in concentrating the energy of others.

Faith is belief in something that cannot be proven. I write this sentence, having faith that the next one will come.

A visionary, at the time of visioning, must strive not to be practical. This does not mean being impractical, but nonpractical. When we consider how a vision might become reality, we inevitably focus on technique rather than on vision and thus *limit* our vision. Faith requires an artist to embrace a vision without knowing exactly how the vision will come alive.

Crises in organizations are often related to faith. We simply do not trust ourselves, one another, our leaders, or the universe. Our political leaders, for example, are among those we trust the least. Many of them have earned our mistrust. However, we, as citizens, have colluded with them. We elect and reelect them, then blame them for our collective failure.

Although we do not elect organizational leaders, we nevertheless collude with them to undermine our faith in ourselves. We ask them to be visionary and too often we denigrate their visions. We ask them to step forward, take charge, be bold, and provide security all at the same time. We ask them for no-risk risks, an impossibility. We want them to lead us into uncharted waters and simultaneously take care of us. They cannot.

Futurist John Naisbitt told us that our culture was shifting from a forty-year reliance on institutions such as the government, the medical establishment, corporations, and school systems, toward a new spirit of self-reliance. Naisbitt wrote, "Somewhere between the shift from institutional help to self-help comes the question 'Can I really do it on my own?' For some people, there is a crisis of confidence, a fear that one is not yet up to the challenge of self-help, perhaps a desire to cling to the comfort of depending on others" (1982, 157).

Can I really do it on my own? Can any of us? M. C. Richards wrote, "We have to trust the invisible gauges we carry within us" (1989, 27). Leaders are experts in conjuring faith — faith in them and faith in ourselves. Leaders trust their invisible gauges and encourage us to trust our own. Leaders inflame our faith in their visions and awaken our faith in who we can be.

THE LEADER'S ARTISTIC MEDIUM

One common way of talking about leadership is to differentiate it from management. In this view, management involves allocating organizational energy: managers historically have decided who works on what tasks. Leadership, on the other hand, involves raising the level of available energy. This does not mean that leaders induce people to work harder or longer, but that they set the context in which people bring all of their energies to a vision. Thus, the artistic medium of a leader is the energy of the followers.

Leaders create by activating the energy of followers, much as a painter activates the energy of paint and a poet activates the energy of words. So leaders must be acquainted with the nature of human energy in the same way that a painter must be acquainted with the spectrum of color. Leaders must discover how to draw all that energy to a point of union, to a focus — to a vision. This is art. Exactly how this is done is the mystery that eludes us when we manufacture lists of leadership behaviors and characteristics. The process is as mysterious as transforming words into poems, paint into images.

If an organization devalues or denies human energy, it restrains leadership. A potential leader in such a situation is like a painter without access to a whole palette or a poet whose vocabulary is impoverished. Leadership is likely to emerge in organizations that are centered. Leadership struggles to emerge in organizations that devalue emotion and spirit and often dies in the struggle.

PRACTICES FOR ARTFUL LEADERS

How might we become artful leaders? Master the processes of vision, of activating and concentrating human energy, and of building faith. Engage in the practices of artists:

- **Separate who you are from who you believe the world wants you to be.**

Leadership and artistry are at least partly about being unlike other people and departing from their expectations. Robert Henri wrote about Walt Whitman, "Nobody wanted Walt Whitman, but Walt Whitman wanted himself, and it is well for us that he did" (1984, 198).

- **Commit to your own growth.**

A leader's growth includes learning the techniques of leadership. That is when lists of leadership behaviors are somewhat useful, much as a poet uses a mental list of forms of poetry or a thesaurus. However, a leader's growth is also about the interior life and about his or her own unique purpose. Technique without purpose and without attention to interior life creates artistry of the surface and superficiality. There are bad poems in all forms.

- **Discover your purpose.**

Every technique ever invented was invented by someone who wanted to fulfill a purpose. A particular technique is attractive to us, and we want to learn it, when we know it has fulfilled its inventor's purpose in another time and place. However, we will only be successful in the technique when we have similar dedication to our own purposes. If we dedicate ourselves to our own purposes we will discover or invent the useful technique for our own time and place. Henry Moore's purpose was to be the greatest sculptor who ever lived and to know it. M. C. Richards sees herself as a "sower of seeds."

- **Trust your intuition and feeling.**

Worship emotion, spirit, and soul along with intellect and rationality. When we do so, we learn, over time, to trust those aspects of ourselves, the fundamental tools of artistry.

- **Express yourself boldly and with passion.**

Much of the art of leadership involves language. Listen to yourself, to the words you use. Are they the words of conformity: "goal," "objective," "strategic plan," "it has come to my attention," "as we informed you"? Where is the passion in those words? Where is the spirit? Speak in words that contain fearless colors.

■ **Develop your appreciation for process as well as product.**

Ask an artist what he or she enjoys about work and, more likely than not, you will hear something about the work process. A painter might point to the flow of paint from brush to canvas, or the mixing of colors. A poet might describe periods of quiet reflection or the creative search for an apt image. A fly-fisherman might recall the *swish, swish* of the line on a long cast.

Leadership is artfulness is process. Leadership is also work; to be artful it must be joyful. The joy is in the process.

■ **Cultivate your willingness to venture into the unknown.**

There are two kinds of unknowns: deep and broad. The deep unknown contains the meaning of a piece of art, the innate significance of a leader's vision, or the spiritual intent of the leader. The deep unknown is the well of meaning beneath the surface of what we already know.

The broad unknown contains lessons from regions we do not normally enter. Leaders are willing to enter new regions, even very strange regions, and bring back what is useful. For example, this book invites leaders into the realm of art to learn lessons that apply to their leadership ability and to their organizations. Several years ago, M. C. Richards began to paint and is now bringing lessons from her painting to her pottery.

- **Accept responsibility for your inspiration and talents.**

One way to discover if you do not take responsibility for your inspiration and talents is by catching yourself avoiding them and feeling guilty later. The cycle of avoidance and guilt often arises from fear: fear that our ideas are not good enough, fear that others will reject our attempts at leadership, fear that we will have to face discouragement, and so on. Accepting responsibility for inspiration and talent usually means sweeping our fear aside.

- **Leap spontaneously between the mundane and the spiritual, and develop centering consciousness.**

These abilities are fundamental to the consciousness of artists and leaders. A poet entertains many considerations when choosing a particular word or image. The primary consideration is, Does this word (or image) carry the spirit of the work in progress? Leaders who grasp that their actions must be "in the same spirit" as their visions will be able to "walk their talk."

- **Discover how to do these things yourself.**

Certainly, artists take classes, study with gurus, and examine the works of masters. However, all artists know that, ultimately, they alone are responsible for their growth.

EPILOGUE

A CREDO FOR
ARTFUL WORK

*To live as artists in the moods
and materials of life!*

I magine we are seated before a glowing fire, or on the bank of a
sparkling stream, or in some other still place. Imagine we are speaking in subdued tones about the sacredness of our work. When at
work, bound as we too often are within rigid angles and uncommit-
ted colors and encased within blank, windowless alcoves, we do not
speak of such things as spirit, soul, joy, desire, fear, passion, hope, despair,
grief, loneliness, meaning, commitment.

Here, at the glowing fire or the sparkling stream, we speak of these
things, aware that everyone experiences them.

We speak of these things, knowing that they reverberate throughout our labor and disturb our souls profoundly, knowing that they penetrate the work of those with whom we share fluorescent conference rooms, strategic plans, balance sheets, and performance appraisals.

118

We speak of these sacred things, before the glowing fire or at the sparkling stream, and we feel unworthy.

We feel unworthy because we feel *soft*. Work is supposed to be *hard*. Labor, toil, a chore, a grind. It takes hard people to do such work. Soft seems dangerous. Yearning for work that is joyful seems naive, almost childish, and definitely soft.

When we as leaders or as workers learn to honor softness, we will deliver the fullness of our energies to our work.

Yet somewhere inside each of us we know that the workplace learns only what we teach it. It embraces only what we carry with us when we enter it.

This is the credo that artful work invites us to carry into our workplaces:

- All work can be artful,
  so I will be artful at work.

- The reward for artful work is in the doing,
  so I will do my work artfully and feel rewarded.

- The ambition of artful work is joy,
  so I will seek joyful work.

- All work is spiritual work,
  so I will work to nurture my spirit.

- To be artful, I must own my work processes,
  so I will claim ownership.

- Artful work requires use of the self,
  so I will use myself — my whole self:
  body, mind, feeling, and spirit —
  in pursuit of centering consciousness.

- As the artist creates the work,
  the work creates the artist,
  so I will acknowledge what is being created
  and encounter what strives to be created.

119

A painter does not normally wait for someone else's permission to start painting or seek another's approval to express feelings. A poet does not normally ask permission to compose or need sanction to give voice to soul. These things happen only in prisons.

The centering of an organization, and the flowering of artful work, begin the instant one person summons the courage to bring one's whole self to the workplace.

REFERENCES

Autry, James A. *Love and Profit: The Art of Caring Leadership*. New York: William Morrow & Company, 1991.

Berman, Morris. *The Reenchantment of the World*. New York: Bantam Books, 1984.

Blanton, Brad. *Radical Honesty: How to Transform Your Life by Telling the Truth*. Stanley, Va.: Sparrowhawk Publications, 1994.

Block, Peter. *Stewardship: Choosing Service over Self-Interest*. San Francisco: Berrett-Koehler, 1993.

Bly, Robert. *Leaping Poetry: An Idea with Poems and Translations*. Boston: Beacon Press, 1975.

Boldt, Laurence. *Zen and the Art of Making a Living: A Practical Guide to Creative Career Design*. New York: Penguin Books, 1993.

Bradshaw, John. *Creating Love: The Next Great Stage of Growth*. New York: Bantam Books, 1994.

Condry, John. "Enemies of Exploration: Self-Initiated Versus Other-Initiated Learning." *Journal of Personality and Social Psychology* 35 (1977): 459–77.

Coomaraswamy, Ananda. *Christian and Oriental Philosophy of Art*. New York: Dover, 1956.

Covey, Steven. *The 7 Habits of Highly Effective People: Powerful Lessons in Personal Change*. New York: Fireside, 1990.

Crosby, Sumner, ed. *Helen Gardner's Art Through the Ages*. New York: Harcourt Brace, 1959.

Csikszentmihalyi, Mihaly. *Flow: The Psychology of Optimal Experience*. New York: HarperPerennial, 1991.

DePree, Max. *Leadership Is an Art*. New York: Dell Publishing, 1989.
———. *Leadership Jazz*. New York: Currency Doubleday, 1992.

Fox, Matthew. *The Reinvention of Work: A New Vision of Livelihood for Our Time*. San Francisco: HarperSanFrancisco, 1994.

Hall, Donald. *Life Work*. Boston: Beacon Press, 1993.

REFERENCES

Heisenberg, Werner. *Physics and Beyond: Encounters and Conversations*. New York: Harper Torchbooks, 1971.

Henri, Robert. *The Art Spirit*. New York: Harper & Row, 1984.

Hillman, James. In *A Blue Fire: Selected Writings by James Hillman,* edited by Thomas Moore, 114–23. New York: Harper & Row, 1989.

Kohn, Alfie. *Punished by Rewards*. Boston: Houghton Mifflin, 1993.

Mack, Alice. *Beyond Turmoil: A Guide to Renewal Through Deep Personal Change*. Tucson, Ariz.: Connexions Unlimited, 1992.

Maclean, Norman. *Young Men and Fire*. Chicago: University of Chicago Press, 1992.

May, Rollo. *The Courage to Create*. New York: Bantam Books, 1975.

Ming-Dao, Deng. *365 Tao: Daily Meditations*. San Francisco: HarperSanFrancisco, 1992.

Moore, Thomas. *Care of the Soul: A Guide for Cultivating Depth and Sacredness in Everyday Life*. New York: HarperCollins, 1992.

Naisbitt, John. *Megatrends: Ten New Directions Transforming Our Lives*. New York: Warner Books, 1982.

Random House College Dictionary, rev. ed. (1975), s.v. "surrender."

Richards, Dick, and Sarah Engel. "After the Vision: Suggestions to Corporate Visionaries and Vision Champions." In Adams, John, ed. *Transforming Leadership*. Alexandria, Va. Miles River Press, 1986.

Richards, Dick, et al. *The Leader Action Inventory*. Sarasota, Fla.: Vector Management Systems, 1988.

Richards, Dick, and Susan Smyth. *Assessing Your Team: 7 Measures of Team Success*. San Diego: Pfeiffer & Company, 1994.

Richards, M. C. *Centering: In Pottery, Poetry, and the Person*. Middletown, Conn.: Wesleyan University Press, 1989.

Robbins, Tom. *Skinny Legs and All*. New York: Bantam Books, 1991.

Saint-Exupéry, Antoine de. *The Little Prince*. New York: Harcourt, 1971.

Vaill, Peter B. *Managing as a Performing Art: New Ideas for a World of Chaotic Change*. San Francisco: Jossey-Bass, 1989.

INDEX

THE AUTHOR

Dick Richards's first career was as a graphic artist. He studied advertising design at the Philadelphia College of Art and has published his photographs, exhibited his paintings and drawings, and performed readings of his poetry. He also taught mathematics and was ombudsman for a suburban school district in eastern Pennsylvania.

Dick has been consulting for nearly twenty years on matters of leadership, creativity, organizational change, career development, and teamwork to companies in the United States, Europe, and Canada. He has consulted with people at all organizational levels in large and small companies, nonprofit organizations, and governmental institutions.

Dick is coauthor, with Susan Smyth, of *Assessing Your Team: 7 Measures of Team Success,* published by Pfeiffer & Company (1994), and *The Leader Action Inventory,* published by Vector Management Systems (1988). In 1986 he cowrote, with Sarah Engel, "After the Vision," an article that gained international recognition from both corporations and university business schools. Dick lives in the Pocono Mountains of Pennsylvania.